MAKE IT FRESH
MAKE IT HEALTHY

We're so excited to share the fresh, healthy and delicious recipes in this cookbook. With *Make It Fresh, Make It Healthy*, eating healthy will never have to be bland or boring again. When the focus is on the natural flavors of fresh ingredients, there's no need to compromise—you can have juicy burgers, creamy risotto or decadent chocolate pie! It's not about what you *can't* eat, it's about making the right choices and finding a balance.

We've taken the guesswork out of healthy eating. You'll be amazed by how easy it can be: just flip through this cookbook, pick a recipe that catches your eye and get cooking! With so many creative options to choose from, you'll find yourself eating fresh and healthy every day!

Enjoy!

The Pampered Chef® Test Kitchens

On the front cover: *Chicken with Fresh Herb Chimichurri*, p. 55.

On the back cover: *Viennese-Style Amaretto Cheesecake*, p. 103.

The Pampered Chef® is the premier direct-seller of high-quality kitchen tools sold through in-home Cooking Shows. We are committed to enhancing family life by providing quality kitchen products supported by service and information for our Consultants and customers.

CONTENTS

LITTLE DISHES

PAGE 6

The satisfying and refreshing recipes in this chapter are great for the times when you don't want a big meal.

MAIN DISHES

PAGE 34

With a wide variety of fresh, inspiring meals to choose from in here, eating healthy has never been easier.

DESSERTS

PAGE 100

Don't skip dessert! Indulge your sweet tooth with these delightfully decadent treats.

"This tastes too good to be good for you!"

When people try the recipes in this cookbook, they're amazed. These recipes not only look beautiful, they *taste* incredible—a "wow" on every page! We set out to create meals and even desserts so tempting, nobody would believe they're good for you. We selected ingredients and techniques to prepare delicious, simple meals guaranteed to impress and satisfy—you won't go hungry with this cookbook around! As always, we made the recipes easier and faster to prepare using our high-quality kitchen tools.

The recipes in this cookbook are mouthwatering, and they also take the guesswork out of healthy eating. The secret? Fresh ingredients within a healthy framework.

So, what is "fresh"?

Just take a walk around the perimeter of your grocery store. That's where the freshest foods are. (Better yet, wander to your local farmers' market. What an inspiring place!) We played with interesting ingredients like fresh fennel, tarragon and figs to add excitement to our recipes. We loaded up on fresh herbs and aromatics such as onions, shallots and garlic to impart bold flavors. The more fresh flavors like these you can pack into a meal, the less fat, salt or sugar you'll need ... or want!

We limited the use of convenience foods to ingredients like dried pastas and grains, purchased unsalted chicken stock, tofu and canned beans. The spotlight in this book is focused on foods that are less processed overall.

What is "healthy" eating?

Below are the nutrients that the American Heart Association® recommends we focus on. These are the recommended *daily* guidelines for an average healthy adult between the ages of 25 and 50 who takes in about 2,000 calories a day. Of course, your specific daily values vary depending on your lifestyle, age and circumstances. For more information about the nutrient values in our recipes, see page 128.

TOTAL FAT – 65 grams or less
(or less than 30% of total calories)

SATURATED FAT – 16 grams or less
(or less than 7% of total fat intake)

CHOLESTEROL – 300 milligrams or less

SODIUM – 1,500 milligrams or less

FIBER – 25-38 grams

For each recipe in this cookbook, we provide nutritional information in a basic nutrition fact panel similar to the one found on packaged products. Remember, the values reflect a *single serving* and are based on a 2,000-calorie diet. Your daily values may be higher or lower depending on your calorie needs.

Nutrition Facts	
Serving Size 2 oz chicken, 1¼ C salad	
Servings Per Recipe 6	

U.S. Nutrients Per Serving	
Calories 410	Calories from Fat 100
	% Daily Value
Total Fat 12g	**18%**
Saturated Fat 2.5g	**13%**
Trans Fat 0g	
Cholesterol 60mg	**20%**
Sodium 480mg	**20%**
Total Carbohydrate 55g	**18%**
Dietary Fiber 5g	**20%**
Sugars 20g	
Protein 25g	

U.S. Diabetic Exchanges Per Serving

3 starch, ½ fruit, 2 medium-fat meat (3½ carb)

How does a 2,000-calorie day add up?

If you follow a typical 3-meal eating pattern each day, you'll have about 500 calories to "spend" on each meal:

Start with a healthy **breakfast** for around 500 calories or less.

For a **light lunch**, choose a recipe from "Little Dishes" for about 250-300 calories. The recipes in this chapter can be easily rounded out with a slice of multigrain bread, if desired.

Select a recipe for **dinner** from our "Main Dish" chapter for 500 calories or less that includes a protein, vegetable and/or grain for a complete meal.

This will allow you to add a couple of **healthy snacks** throughout the day for an additional 200 calories.

Then, to top it off, you can even choose a **treat** from "Desserts" for as low as 200-300 calories!

We've done the thinking for you

The bottom line is that preparing fresh, healthy and satisfying recipes doesn't have to be hard! By making the recipes in this cookbook, you'll automatically be putting some good cooking habits into practice. Here are just a few examples of healthier ingredient choices and cooking techniques found in this book that will help you to cook and eat more healthfully.

- We started with quick-cooking whole grain barley and vegetables to pack *Loaded Baked Tomatoes* (at left and on p. 29) with nutrients and fiber, making them deliciously satisfying.

- For a low-calorie alternative to bread, we used lettuce leaves to hold a tasty couscous, turkey and garbanzo bean salad for *Mediterranean Lettuce Wraps* (at left and on p. 57).

- To satisfy your sweet tooth, we used meringue in the lemony cupcake batter and luscious frosting for *Lemon Chiffon Cupcakes* (at left and on p. 107) to make them seem sinfully decadent without adding much fat.

Little changes add up

Remember, you don't have to tackle your entire diet in order to see improvements in your health. Little changes add up to big differences. Even if you find a few favorite recipes in this cookbook, you'll be on the right track. Start by flipping through the pages and flagging recipes that excite you. Out of those, choose the one you want to do first, and go for it!

LITTLE DISHES

3	cups (750 mL) unsalted chicken stock
¼	tsp (1 mL) saffron threads
3	medium shallots
1½	tbsp (22 mL) olive oil
1	cup (250 mL) uncooked Arborio rice
¾	cup (175 mL) dry white wine such as Sauvignon Blanc
8	oz (250 g) fresh asparagus spears, trimmed and cut diagonally into 1-in. (2.5-cm) pieces
2	oz (60 g) Parmesan cheese, grated (½ cup/125 mL), divided
½	tsp (2 mL) salt
½	tsp (2 mL) coarsely ground black pepper
1	oz (30 g) reduced-fat cream cheese (Neufchâtel)

Nutrition Facts

Serving Size ⅔ C risotto
Servings Per Recipe 6

U.S. Nutrients Per Serving

Calories 240	Calories from Fat 60

	% Daily Value
Total Fat 7g	11%
Saturated Fat 2.5g	13%
Trans Fat 0g	
Cholesterol 10mg	3%
Sodium 380mg	16%
Total Carbohydrate 30g	10%
Dietary Fiber 2g	8%
Sugars 1g	
Protein 10g	

U.S. Diabetic Exchanges Per Serving

2 starch, 1 vegetable, 1 fat (2 carb)

Creamy Saffron & Asparagus Risotto

Saffron adds an exotic accent to this elegantly simple risotto.

PREP TIME: 20 MINUTES   TOTAL TIME: 35 MINUTES   YIELD: 6 SERVINGS

1 In (1.5-qt./1.4-L) Saucepan, bring stock and saffron to a simmer over medium heat. Reduce heat to low.

2 Meanwhile, finely chop shallots using Food Chopper. In (10-in./24-cm) Skillet, cook oil and shallots over medium heat 1-2 minutes or until fragrant. Add rice; cook and stir 1 minute or until rice is evenly coated with oil. Add wine; cook 3-4 minutes or until wine is evaporated, stirring often with Bamboo Spoon.

3 Using Ladle, pour ½ cup (125 mL) of the hot stock into Skillet. Cook 2-3 minutes or until stock is absorbed, stirring constantly. Repeat with remaining stock in ½-cup (125-mL) increments, cooking and stirring 2-3 minutes after each addition until all but ½ cup (125 mL) of the stock has been added (15-17 minutes total cook time).

4 Add remaining ½ cup (125 mL) stock, asparagus, ⅓ cup (75 mL) of the Parmesan cheese, salt and black pepper to Skillet. Cook 3-4 minutes or until asparagus is crisp-tender, stirring occasionally. Remove Skillet from heat. Add cream cheese and stir until incorporated. Divide risotto among serving bowls and sprinkle with remaining Parmesan cheese.

Cook's Tip

Keeping the stock hot during cooking ensures that the rice cooks evenly by not allowing the temperature of the rice to drop. Adding the saffron to the stock first gives the saffron time to infuse its exotic fragrance and yellow hue into the risotto.

- 2 boneless, skinless chicken breasts (4 oz/125 g each)
- ¼ tsp (1 mL) plus ⅛ tsp (0.5 mL) salt, divided
- ⅛ tsp (0.5 mL) coarsely ground black pepper
- ¼ cup (50 mL) light mayonnaise
- 2 tbsp (30 mL) red wine vinegar
- 2 tbsp (30 mL) chopped fresh tarragon leaves
- 1 tbsp (15 mL) light brown sugar
- 8 oz (250 g) fresh green beans, trimmed
- ½ medium jicama (about 10 oz/300 g)
- 1 medium Granny Smith apple
- 3 cups (750 mL) mixed greens salad blend

  Additional coarsely ground black pepper (optional)

Nutrition Facts

Serving Size 1 C salad, ½ C greens
Servings Per Recipe 6

U.S. Nutrients Per Serving

Calories 120	Calories from Fat 30
	% Daily Value
Total Fat 3.5g	5%
Saturated Fat 0.5g	3%
Trans Fat 0g	
Cholesterol 25mg	8%
Sodium 260mg	11%
Total Carbohydrate 14g	5%
Dietary Fiber 4g	16%
Sugars 8g	
Protein 9g	

U.S. Diabetic Exchanges Per Serving

½ fruit, 1 vegetable, 1½ low-fat meat (½ carb)

Chicken, Green Bean & Apple Salad

This crisp, cold salad is perfect for a hot summer day, but it's so delicious, you're sure to enjoy it in any season!

PREP TIME: 15 MINUTES   **TOTAL TIME:** 30 MINUTES   **YIELD:** 6 SERVINGS

1 Heat **Grill Pan** over medium heat 5 minutes. Spray with canola oil using **Kitchen Spritzer**. Sprinkle chicken with ⅛ tsp (0.5 mL) of the salt and black pepper. Place chicken into pan and top with **Grill Press**. Cook 5 minutes on each side or until internal temperature reaches 165°F (74°C) and grill marks appear. Place chicken on a plate and refrigerate until ready to use.

2 Meanwhile, for dressing, combine mayonnaise, vinegar, tarragon, brown sugar and remaining ¼ tsp (1 mL) salt in **Small Batter Bowl**. Whisk using **Stainless Whisk**. Cover and refrigerate.

3 Fill **Classic Batter Bowl** halfway with ice water; set aside. Place green beans and ¼ cup (50 mL) water into **Large Micro-Cooker®**. Microwave, covered, on HIGH 2-3 minutes or until beans are crisp-tender; drain and immediately plunge into ice water. Let stand 5 minutes; drain and pat dry with paper towels. Meanwhile, peel jicama using **Serrated Peeler**. Slice jicama using **Ultimate Mandoline** fitted with adjustable slicing blade on thick setting. Cut slices into strips using **Santoku Knife**. Core and thinly slice apple.

4 Remove chicken from refrigerator; slice crosswise into strips. Combine chicken, dressing, beans, jicama and apple in **Stainless (4-qt./4-L) Mixing Bowl**; toss gently. Serve salad with mixed greens and garnish with additional black pepper, if desired.

Cook's Tip

Tarragon is a leafy herb with an assertive anise flavor. It has pointed dark leaves and is used in French cooking.

- 1 cup (250 mL) loosely packed fresh basil leaves
- 1 lemon, divided
- 3 tbsp (45 mL) light mayonnaise
- 3 garlic cloves, pressed, divided
- ¼ tsp (1 mL) sugar
- ⅛ tsp (0.5 mL) salt
- 2 tsp (10 mL) olive oil
- 8 oz (250 g) medium uncooked shrimp (26-30 per pound), peeled and deveined, tails removed
- ¼ tsp (1 mL) coarsely ground black pepper
- 2 pita pocket bread rounds, cut in half
- 2 plum tomatoes
- 2 cups (500 mL) fresh baby spinach leaves
- ½ small cantaloupe, thinly sliced

Nutrition Facts

Serving Size 1 filled pita, 3 slices cantaloupe
Servings Per Recipe 4

U.S. Nutrients Per Serving

Calories 220	Calories from Fat 60
	% Daily Value
Total Fat 6g	9%
Saturated Fat 1g	5%
Trans Fat 0g	
Cholesterol 90mg	30%
Sodium 440mg	18%
Total Carbohydrate 26g	9%
Dietary Fiber 2g	8%
Sugars 5g	
Protein 16g	

U.S. Diabetic Exchanges Per Serving

1 starch, ½ fruit, 1 vegetable, 1½ low-fat meat (1½ carb)

Grilled Shrimp Pitas with Basil Aioli

Lemon and basil punch up the flavor in these quick sandwiches.

PREP TIME: 15 MINUTES   **TOTAL TIME:** 25 MINUTES   **YIELD:** 4 SERVINGS

1 Finely chop basil using **Chef's Knife**. Zest lemon using **Microplane® Zester** to measure 1 tsp (5 mL). Juice lemon to measure 1 tsp (5 mL). For aioli, combine basil, zest, mayonnaise and one of the pressed garlic cloves in **Classic Batter Bowl**; mix well and set aside. For vinaigrette, combine lemon juice, sugar and salt in **(1-cup/250-mL) Prep Bowl**. Slowly add oil, whisking until well blended. Set aside.

2 Combine shrimp, black pepper and remaining pressed garlic in **Small Batter Bowl**; mix well. Heat **Grill Pan** over medium-high heat 5 minutes. Spray with olive oil using **Kitchen Spritzer**. Place two of the pita halves in pan, top with **Grill Press** and cook 20-30 seconds or until grill marks appear. Turn pitas over; top with press and cook an additional 30 seconds or until grill marks appear. Repeat with remaining pitas; wrap in foil to keep warm. Add shrimp to pan, top with press and cook 2-3 minutes or until shrimp are opaque (do not turn shrimp). Add shrimp to aioli; mix well.

3 Meanwhile, slice tomatoes crosswise. Combine spinach and vinaigrette in small **Colander Bowl**; toss gently. To assemble, fill pita halves with spinach, tomatoes and shrimp; serve with cantaloupe slices.

Cook's Tip

Aioli is a garlic-flavored mayonnaise that is a popular condiment for fish and shellfish.

1	small eggplant (about 1 lb/450 g), peeled
1	medium red bell pepper
1	small red onion
½	cup (125 mL) loosely packed fresh basil leaves, divided
½	tsp (2 mL) plus ⅛ tsp (0.5 mL) salt, divided
½	loaf Italian bread (8 oz/250 g)
	Garlic Oil or olive oil
2	tsp (10 mL) olive oil
3	garlic cloves, pressed
3	tbsp (45 mL) red wine vinegar, divided
½	tsp (2 mL) coarsely ground black pepper, divided
2	oz (60 g) smoked mozzarella cheese, shredded
1	seedless cucumber
1	tbsp (15 mL) chopped fresh mint leaves
1	tsp (5 mL) sugar

Nutrition Facts
Serving Size 3 bruschetta, about ¼ C salad
Servings Per Recipe 6

U.S. Nutrients Per Serving

Calories 180	Calories from Fat 50
	% Daily Value
Total Fat 6g	**9%**
Saturated Fat 2g	**10%**
Trans Fat 0g	
Cholesterol 10mg	**3%**
Sodium 480mg	**20%**
Total Carbohydrate 25g	**8%**
Dietary Fiber 4g	**16%**
Sugars 4g	
Protein 7g	

U.S. Diabetic Exchanges Per Serving

1 starch, 2 vegetable, 1 fat (1 carb)

Smoky Eggplant Bruschetta

A small amount of smoked mozzarella adds a big burst of flavor.

PREP TIME: 25 MINUTES   **TOTAL TIME:** 45 MINUTES   **YIELD:** 6 SERVINGS

1 Preheat oven to 425°F (220°C). Dice eggplant, bell pepper and onion using **Chef's Knife**. Thinly slice basil. Set aside bell pepper, onion and basil. Place eggplant into small **Colander** and sprinkle with ¼ tsp (1 mL) of the salt; toss gently and let stand 15 minutes.

2 Slice bread into eighteen ¼-inch-thick (6-mm) slices. Arrange bread over **Large Round Stone with Handles**. Lightly spray with Garlic Oil using **Kitchen Spritzer** and bake 9-11 minutes or until edges begin to brown. Remove baking stone from oven to **Stackable Cooling Rack**.

3 Meanwhile, heat olive oil in **(12-in./30-cm) Skillet** over medium-high heat 1-3 minutes or until shimmering. Add eggplant; cook undisturbed 3-4 minutes or until browned. Add bell pepper and onion; cook and stir 3-4 minutes or until vegetables are tender. Add pressed garlic and cook 20-30 seconds or until fragrant.

4 Remove Skillet from heat. Reserve 2 tbsp (30 mL) basil for garnish. Stir in remaining basil, ¼ tsp (1 mL) of the salt, 2 tbsp (30 mL) of the vinegar and ¼ tsp (1 mL) of the black pepper. Top bread with vegetable mixture and cheese. Bake 4-5 minutes or until cheese is melted. Garnish with reserved basil.

5 Meanwhile, cut cucumber in half lengthwise; remove core using **Core & More** and thinly slice crosswise. Place cucumber, mint, sugar, remaining ⅛ tsp (0.5 mL) salt, remaining 1 tbsp (15 mL) vinegar and remaining ¼ tsp (1 mL) black pepper in **Classic Batter Bowl**; mix well. Serve salad with bruschetta.

Cook's Tips

Choose a good-quality Italian bread that is crusty on the outside and tender on the inside for best results.

Sprinkling the eggplant with salt removes excess moisture from the eggplant to ensure better browning while sautéing.

CRAB SALAD

- 6 oz (175 g) cooked king crabmeat (about 12 oz/350 g crab legs in shells)
- ¼ small red onion
- 1 jalapeño pepper, stemmed and seeded
- ¼ cup (50 mL) loosely packed fresh cilantro
- 2 limes, divided
- ¼ tsp (1 mL) coarsely ground black pepper

MANGO PUREE

- 1 seedless cucumber, divided
- 2 large mangoes, peeled and cut into chunks
- ¼ cup (50 mL) sweet white wine such as Riesling
- 3 tbsp (45 mL) honey
- 1 tbsp (15 mL) fresh lime juice (from lime used in salad)

Nutrition Facts

Serving Size ⅓ C salad, ½ C puree
Servings Per Recipe 4

U.S. Nutrients Per Serving

Calories 180	Calories from Fat 10

	% Daily Value
Total Fat 1g	2%
Saturated Fat 0g	0%
Trans Fat 0g	
Cholesterol 25mg	8%
Sodium 460mg	19%
Total Carbohydrate 34g	11%
Dietary Fiber 3g	12%
Sugars 30g	
Protein 10g	

U.S. Diabetic Exchanges Per Serving

2 fruit, 1 vegetable, 1 low-fat meat (2 carb)

Cool Crab Cocktails with Mango Puree

Mango and cucumber puree is a cool and refreshing backdrop for zesty crab salad.

PREP TIME: 20 MINUTES   **TOTAL TIME:** 1 HOUR   **YIELD:** 4 SERVINGS

1 For salad, remove crabmeat from shells (see Cook's Tip) and place in **Classic Batter Bowl**. Using **Food Chopper**, finely chop onion and jalapeño; coarsely chop cilantro. Juice limes using **Citrus Press** to measure 1½ tbsp (22 mL); set aside 1 tbsp (15 mL) of the juice for mango puree. Add onion, jalapeño, cilantro, ½ tbsp (7 mL) of the remaining lime juice and black pepper to batter bowl. Gently toss salad with **Mix 'N Scraper®**. Refrigerate 30 minutes.

2 For puree, cut cucumber in half; set aside half for later use. Cut remaining cucumber half into thirds. Place cucumber, mangoes, wine, honey and lime juice into blender container; cover and blend until smooth. Refrigerate 30-45 minutes or until chilled.

3 Cut reserved cucumber half diagonally into ¼-in. (6-mm) slices. Divide puree evenly among four **Dots Martini Glasses**; top with salad. Garnish with cucumber slices.

Cook's Tip

Using **Professional Shears**, carefully cut down length of shell on two opposite sides of crab leg; split shell apart to remove meat.

- 4 large portobello mushrooms with stems (4-5-in./10-13-cm diameter), divided
- ½ cup (125 mL) uncooked quinoa
- 1 cup (250 mL) vegetable broth
- 3 tbsp (45 mL) balsamic vinegar, divided
- 1 small zucchini
- ¾ cup (175 mL) canned quartered artichoke hearts, drained
- 4 green onions with tops
- 2 plum tomatoes
- 2 oz (60 g) Asiago cheese
- 2 tbsp (30 mL) chopped fresh basil leaves
- 1 garlic clove, pressed
- ¼ tsp (1 mL) coarsely ground black pepper
- 4 cups (1 L) mixed greens salad blend

Nutrition Facts

Serving Size 1 filled mushroom, 1 C greens
Servings Per Recipe 4

U.S. Nutrients Per Serving

Calories 210	Calories from Fat 60

	% Daily Value
Total Fat 6g	9%
Saturated Fat 2.5g	13%
Trans Fat 0g	
Cholesterol 15mg	5%
Sodium 400mg	17%
Total Carbohydrate 29g	10%
Dietary Fiber 6g	24%
Sugars 7g	
Protein 10g	

U.S. Diabetic Exchanges Per Serving

1½ starch, 1½ vegetable, 1 fat (1½ carb)

Quinoa-Stuffed Portobello Mushrooms

This meatless dish features an array of vegetables and is sure to satisfy.

PREP TIME: 20 MINUTES   **TOTAL TIME:** 40 MINUTES   **YIELD:** 4 SERVINGS

1. Preheat oven to 375°F (190°C). Line **Large Sheet Pan** with foil. Remove stems from mushrooms; set caps aside. Chop mushroom stems to measure ½ cup (125 mL) using **Food Chopper**. Place quinoa in **(7-in./18-cm) Strainer** and rinse under cold water 30 seconds. Bring broth to a boil in **(2-qt./1.9-L) Saucepan** over medium-high heat; add quinoa and mushroom stems. Reduce heat to medium; simmer, covered, 15 minutes or until liquid is absorbed. Place quinoa mixture in **Classic Batter Bowl**.

2. Meanwhile, remove and discard brown gills from the undersides of mushroom caps (see Cook's Tip). Place mushrooms, rounded side down, onto pan. Place 5 tsp (25 mL) of the vinegar in **(1-cup/250-mL) Prep Bowl**; brush generously over both sides of mushrooms using **Chef's Silicone Basting Brush**.

3. For filling, chop zucchini using **Santoku Knife**. Thinly slice artichokes and green onions. Seed and dice tomatoes. Grate cheese using **Rotary Grater**. Add zucchini, artichokes, onions, tomatoes, cheese, basil, pressed garlic, black pepper and 1 tsp (5 mL) of the vinegar to quinoa mixture; toss thoroughly to combine.

4. Spoon filling evenly into mushrooms. Bake 20-25 minutes or until mushrooms are tender. Place mixed greens and remaining 1 tbsp (15 mL) vinegar in **Stainless (2-qt./2-L) Mixing Bowl**; toss to coat. Serve mushrooms with mixed greens.

Cook's Tips

To clean mushrooms, wipe them with a damp paper towel. To prevent mushrooms from becoming soggy, do not clean them until ready to use.

When removing brown gills from underside of mushrooms, leave a small amount of the gills around the outer edge. This will help keep the mushroom caps intact when baking.

3-4	limes
3	tbsp (45 mL) honey
1	tbsp (15 mL) snipped fresh chives
⅛	tsp (0.5 mL) cayenne pepper

SALAD

½	small jicama (about 1 cup/250 mL strips)
½	small seedless watermelon (about 4 cups/1 L strips)
½	seedless cucumber (about 1½ cups/375 mL slices)
4	large Boston lettuce leaves
2½	oz (75 g) prosciutto, thinly sliced
½	oz (15 g) feta cheese, crumbled
1	tbsp (15 mL) snipped fresh chives
	Cayenne pepper (optional)

Nutrition Facts

Serving Size ⅔ oz prosciutto, 1½ C salad
Servings Per Recipe 4

U.S. Nutrients Per Serving

Calories 170	Calories from Fat 30
	% Daily Value
Total Fat 3.5g	5%
Saturated Fat 1.5g	8%
Trans Fat 0g	
Cholesterol 20mg	7%
Sodium 400mg	17%
Total Carbohydrate 31g	10%
Dietary Fiber 4g	16%
Sugars 23g	
Protein 8g	

U.S. Diabetic Exchanges Per Serving

2 fruit, 1 low-fat meat (2 carb)

Watermelon & Prosciutto Salad

The salty and sweet ingredients in this salad complement each other perfectly.

PREP TIME: 20 MINUTES   **TOTAL TIME:** 20 MINUTES   **YIELD:** 4 SERVINGS

1 For dressing, using **Microplane® Zester**, zest one lime to measure 1 tsp (5 mL). Using **Citrus Press**, juice limes to measure ¼ cup (50 mL). Combine zest, juice, honey, chives and cayenne pepper in **(1-cup/250-mL) Easy Read Measuring Cup**; whisk with **Stainless Mini Whisk** until blended. Refrigerate until chilled.

2 For salad, peel jicama with **Serrated Peeler**. Cut jicama and watermelon into strips with **Santoku Knife**. Slice cucumber using **Ultimate Mandoline** fitted with v-shaped blade; cut slices in half.

3 Place jicama, watermelon and cucumber in **Stainless (4-qt./4-L) Mixing Bowl**. Pour dressing over salad; mix gently with **Mix 'N Scraper®**.

4 To serve, divide lettuce leaves among serving plates; top with salad and prosciutto. Sprinkle with cheese, chives and cayenne pepper, if desired.

Cook's Tip

Prosciutto is a dry-cured ham that is usually thinly sliced. It can be found in the deli section of most grocery stores.

6 uncooked manicotti pasta shells

1 lemon, divided

2 cans (5 oz or 170 g each) very low-sodium solid white albacore tuna in water, drained

½ cup (125 mL) light mayonnaise

¼ cup (50 mL) chopped fresh parsley, divided

¼ small red onion, finely chopped

3 tbsp (45 mL) capers, drained, divided

1 tsp (5 mL) coarsely ground black pepper, divided

3 medium vine-ripened tomatoes

Nutrition Facts

Serving Size 1 cannelloni, ⅓ C relish
Servings Per Recipe 6

U.S. Nutrients Per Serving

Calories 170	Calories from Fat 50
	% Daily Value
Total Fat 6g	9%
Saturated Fat 1g	5%
Trans Fat 0g	
Cholesterol 25mg	8%
Sodium 320mg	13%
Total Carbohydrate 18g	6%
Dietary Fiber 2g	8%
Sugars 3g	
Protein 14g	

U.S. Diabetic Exchanges Per Serving

1 starch, ½ vegetable, 1½ low-fat meat (1 carb)

Tuna Cannelloni with Tomato-Caper Relish

Tuna salad is dressed up with capers, lemon zest and fresh parsley and served in cool cannelloni shells. The result is a classic Spanish tapas dish.

PREP TIME: 15 MINUTES   **TOTAL TIME:** 25 MINUTES   **YIELD:** 6 SERVINGS

1 Cook pasta shells according to package directions, omitting salt and oil and cooking an additional 1-2 minutes or until pasta is completely tender. Using **Chef's Tongs**, carefully transfer pasta to large **Colander** and gently rinse under cold water. Set aside.

2 Meanwhile, for filling, zest lemon using **Microplane® Zester** to measure 1 tsp (5 mL). Juice lemon using **Juicer** to measure 1 tbsp (15 mL); set aside. Combine zest, tuna, mayonnaise, 2 tbsp (30 mL) of the parsley, onion, 1 tbsp (15 mL) of the capers and ½ tsp (2 mL) of the black pepper in **Classic Batter Bowl**; mix well. Spoon filling into large resealable plastic bag; set aside.

3 For relish, core and seed tomatoes using **Core & More**. Finely dice tomatoes using **Chef's Knife**. Combine tomatoes, lemon juice, remaining 2 tbsp (30 mL) parsley, remaining 2 tbsp (30 mL) capers and remaining ½ tsp (2 mL) black pepper in **Small Batter Bowl**; mix well.

4 To assemble cannelloni, trim corner of bag containing filling using **Professional Shears**. Pipe filling into pasta shells. Serve cannelloni with relish.

Cook's Tip

When purchasing manicotti shells, check to make sure they are not broken.

TOAST & SALAD

- 4 slices white sandwich bread, crusts removed
- 4 slices turkey bacon, divided (see Cook's Tip)
- 3 plum tomatoes
- ¼ tsp (1 mL) coarsely ground black pepper
- ⅔ cup (150 mL) panko bread crumbs
- 2 tbsp (30 mL) all-purpose flour
- ¼ cup (50 mL) pasteurized refrigerated egg product
- 2 heads iceberg lettuce, sliced ¾ in. (2 cm) thick (see Cook's Tip)
- 2 tbsp (30 mL) snipped fresh chives

DRESSING

- ⅔ cup (150 mL) low-fat buttermilk
- 3½ tbsp (52 mL) light mayonnaise
- 1 garlic clove, pressed
- ¼ tsp (1 mL) coarsely ground black pepper
- 2 tbsp (30 mL) snipped fresh chives
- 2 tbsp (30 mL) finely chopped cooked turkey bacon from salad

Nutrition Facts

Serving Size 1 serving, ¼ C dressing
Servings Per Recipe 4

U.S. Nutrients Per Serving

Calories 200	Calories from Fat 60
	% Daily Value
Total Fat 7g	11%
Saturated Fat 1.5g	8%
Trans Fat 0g	
Cholesterol 15mg	5%
Sodium 420mg	18%
Total Carbohydrate 26g	9%
Dietary Fiber 2g	8%
Sugars 6g	
Protein 9g	

U.S. Diabetic Exchanges Per Serving

1½ starch, 1 vegetable, 1 fat (1½ carb)

Guiltless BLT Salad

Here's a new way to enjoy the popular combination of bacon, lettuce and tomato.

PREP TIME: 20 MINUTES **TOTAL TIME:** 30 MINUTES **YIELD:** 4 SERVINGS

1 Preheat oven to 400°F (200°C). Cut bread in half diagonally; lightly spray with canola oil using **Kitchen Spritzer**. Arrange bread on **Medium Round Stone with Handles**; bake 12-14 minutes or until golden brown. Remove baking stone from oven to **Stackable Cooling Rack**; set aside.

2 Cook bacon in **Executive (10-in./24-cm) Skillet** (do not use stainless cookware) over medium-high heat 6-8 minutes or until crisp. Remove from Skillet and cool slightly. Finely chop bacon with **Food Chopper**; set aside. Cut tomatoes into 12 slices. Blot excess moisture from tomatoes with paper towels; sprinkle with black pepper. Place bread crumbs into one **Coating Tray**; microwave on HIGH 2-3 minutes or until golden brown, stirring every 30 seconds. Place flour into second tray and egg product into third tray. Lightly dredge each tomato slice in flour; dip into egg product and then into bread crumbs, coating evenly.

3 Spray same Skillet with canola oil; heat over medium-high heat 1-3 minutes or until shimmering. Cook tomato slices 2-3 minutes on each side or until deep golden brown; remove Skillet from heat.

4 For dressing, combine buttermilk, mayonnaise, pressed garlic and black pepper in **Small Batter Bowl**. Whisk until smooth; stir in chives and 2 tbsp (30 mL) of the bacon. To serve, divide lettuce slices among serving plates; top with three tomato slices. Drizzle with dressing and garnish with remaining bacon and chives. Serve with toast.

Cook's Tips

Choose turkey bacon that has 65% less fat than regular bacon and contains about 135 mg sodium per slice.

For the prettiest presentation, keep the lettuce slices intact (don't separate into individual leaves) after slicing.

Panko are Japanese-style bread crumbs that can be found in the ethnic section of most grocery stores.

1 seedless cucumber

½ cup (125 mL) loosely packed
   fresh parsley

2 cups (500 mL) grape tomatoes

½ tsp (2 mL) coarsely ground
   black pepper, divided

⅓ cup (75 mL) rice vinegar

1 tbsp (15 mL) olive oil

2 tsp (10 mL) sugar

1 garlic clove, pressed

FALAFEL & RICE

2 cans (15 oz or 398 mL each) no-salt-
   added garbanzo beans

1 medium onion, quartered

½ cup (125 mL) *each* loosely packed
   fresh parsley and cilantro

½ cup (125 mL) all-purpose flour

¼ cup (50 mL) pasteurized refrigerated
   egg product

1 tbsp (15 mL) ground cumin, toasted

2 garlic cloves, peeled

¾ tsp (4 mL) *each* salt and coarsely
   ground black pepper

1 tbsp (15 mL) olive oil, divided

1½ cups (375 mL) cooked basmati rice
   (see Cook's Tip)

Baked Falafel with Jerusalem Salad

Falafel, which are hearty, meatless patties, are usually breaded and deep fried. Our baked version is just as satisfying.

PREP TIME: 45 MINUTES   **TOTAL TIME:** 1 HOUR   **YIELD:** 6 SERVINGS

1 Preheat oven to 400°F (200°C). For salad, slice cucumber using **Ultimate Mandoline** fitted with adjustable blade on thick setting; cut slices in half using **Utility Knife**. Coarsely chop parsley. Cut tomatoes in half lengthwise. Combine cucumber, parsley, tomatoes and ¼ tsp (1 mL) of the black pepper in **Stainless (4-qt./4-L) Mixing Bowl**. For vinaigrette, whisk together vinegar, oil, sugar, pressed garlic and remaining ¼ tsp (1 mL) black pepper in **(2-cup/500-mL) Prep Bowl**. Reserve 2 tbsp (30 mL) for later use in sauce, if desired (see Cook's Tip). Add remaining vinaigrette to salad; stir to coat. Refrigerate 30 minutes, stirring occasionally.

2 For falafel, drain and rinse beans using large **Colander**. Place beans in food processor; cover and pulse until coarsely pureed, occasionally scraping down sides of bowl. Transfer beans to **Classic Batter Bowl**. Combine onion, herbs, flour, egg product, cumin, garlic, salt and black pepper in food processor; cover and pulse until finely chopped. Add onion mixture to beans; mix well.

3 Brush **Large Sheet Pan** with ½ tbsp (7 mL) of the oil using **Chef's Silicone Basting Brush**. Using rounded **Large Scoop**, drop 12 scoops of falafel mixture onto pan, spacing 1½ in. (4 cm) apart; slightly flatten with back of scoop. Brush tops of patties with remaining oil. Bake 20–25 minutes or until golden brown, turning once; remove pan from oven to **Stackable Cooling Rack**. Serve patties with salad and rice; drizzle with sauce, if desired.

Cook's Tips

To make basmati rice, prepare ¾ cup (175 mL) uncooked rice according to package directions, omitting salt, butter or oil.

To make a tangy sauce, in **(1-cup/250-mL) Prep Bowl**, combine ¼ cup (50 mL) reduced-fat sour cream and 2 tbsp (30 mL) of the vinaigrette from salad.

Nutrition Facts

Serving Size 2 patties, 1 C salad, ¼ C rice
Servings Per Recipe 6

U.S. Nutrients Per Serving

Calories 280	Calories from Fat 50

	% Daily Value
Total Fat 5g	8%
Saturated Fat 0.5g	3%
Trans Fat 0g	
Cholesterol 0mg	0%
Sodium 340mg	14%
Total Carbohydrate 47g	16%
Dietary Fiber 6g	24%
Sugars 5g	
Protein 10g	

U.S. Diabetic Exchanges Per Serving

3 starch, 1 fat (3 carb)

- ¾ cup (175 mL) uncooked quick-cooking barley
- 6 large firm, ripe tomatoes
- 5 slices turkey bacon (see Cook's Tip)
- 3 large shallots
- 8 oz (250 g) fresh crimini mushrooms
- 2 garlic cloves, pressed
- 1 tbsp (15 mL) finely chopped fresh thyme leaves
- 6 cups (1.5 L) fresh baby spinach leaves (6 oz/175 g)
- ¾ cup (175 mL) grated fresh Parmesan cheese (3 oz/90 g), divided
- ¾ tsp (4 mL) coarsely ground black pepper, divided
- ¼ tsp (1 mL) salt

Nutrition Facts

Serving Size 1 filled tomato
Servings Per Recipe 6

U.S. Nutrients Per Serving

Calories 230	Calories from Fat 50
	% Daily Value
Total Fat 6g	9%
Saturated Fat 2.5g	13%
Trans Fat 0g	
Cholesterol 20mg	7%
Sodium 390mg	16%
Total Carbohydrate 34g	11%
Dietary Fiber 8g	32%
Sugars 6g	
Protein 13g	

U.S. Diabetic Exchanges Per Serving

2 starch, 1 vegetable, ½ high-fat meat (2 carb)

Loaded Baked Tomatoes

Barley, turkey bacon and mushrooms provide a smoky, hearty filling in a colorful tomato cup.

PREP TIME: 15 MINUTES　　**TOTAL TIME:** 35 MINUTES　　**YIELD:** 6 SERVINGS

1　Preheat broiler on HIGH. Prepare barley according to package directions, omitting salt. Set aside. Using **Color Coated Tomato Knife**, slice stem end off of tomatoes. Remove and discard pulp and seeds using **Core & More**. Place tomatoes cut-side down on paper towel-lined **Medium Sheet Pan**; set aside.

2　Meanwhile, cook bacon in **(12-in./30-cm) Skillet** over medium-high heat 6-8 minutes or until crisp; remove from Skillet. Finely chop bacon and shallots with **Food Chopper**; set aside. Thinly slice mushrooms. Spray Skillet with canola oil using **Kitchen Spritzer**. Heat over medium-high heat 1-3 minutes or until shimmering. Sauté mushrooms 6-8 minutes or until browned, stirring occasionally. Add shallots, pressed garlic and thyme; sauté 1-2 minutes or until shallots are tender. Add barley, bacon and spinach to Skillet; cook 1-2 minutes or until spinach is wilted, stirring occasionally. Remove Skillet from heat. Stir in ½ cup (125 mL) of the cheese, ½ tsp (2 mL) of the black pepper and salt.

3　Remove paper towels from pan; arrange tomatoes cut-side up on pan and sprinkle with remaining ¼ tsp (1 mL) black pepper. Using **Medium Scoop**, scoop barley mixture evenly into tomatoes; sprinkle with remaining cheese. Place pan 3-4 in. (7.5-10 cm) from heating element. Broil tomatoes 20-30 seconds or until cheese is melted. Carefully remove pan from oven; serve tomatoes immediately.

Cook's Tips

Choose turkey bacon with 65% less fat than regular bacon and contains about 135 mg sodium per slice.

If necessary, to make tomatoes stand upright in pan, slice off a thin piece from bottom of tomato, creating a flat base.

Ingredients

- 8 slices (1 oz/30 g each) whole grain baguette, divided
- 2 tsp (10 mL) olive oil
- ½ tsp (2 mL) coarsely ground black pepper, divided
- 1 seedless cucumber, divided
- 1 medium red onion, divided
- 1 jalapeño pepper, stemmed and seeded, divided
- 4 plum tomatoes, seeded
- 2 cups (500 mL) diced seedless watermelon
- 1½ cups (375 mL) loosely packed fresh cilantro, chopped, divided
- 1 large red bell pepper
- 1 can (14.5 oz) no-salt-added diced tomatoes, undrained (about 1¾ cups/425 mL)
- 1 cup (250 mL) low-sodium vegetable juice, chilled
- 2 tbsp (30 mL) sherry vinegar
- 2 garlic cloves, pressed
- ⅛ tsp (0.5 mL) salt

Nutrition Facts

Serving Size 1⅓ C gazpacho, 1 slice bread
Servings Per Recipe 6

U.S. Nutrients Per Serving

Calories 180	Calories from Fat 30

	% Daily Value
Total Fat 3.5g	5%
Saturated Fat 0.5g	3%
Trans Fat 0g	
Cholesterol 0mg	0%
Sodium 250mg	10%
Total Carbohydrate 33g	11%
Dietary Fiber 6g	24%
Sugars 14g	
Protein 8g	

U.S. Diabetic Exchanges Per Serving

1½ starch, 2 vegetable, ½ fat (1½ carb)

Cool Gazpacho with Watermelon

Fresh watermelon adds a subtle sweetness to this refreshing chilled Spanish soup.

PREP TIME: 20 MINUTES   **TOTAL TIME:** 1 HOUR, 20 MINUTES   **YIELD:** 6 SERVINGS

1 Preheat oven to 425°F (220°C). Brush six of the bread slices with oil using **Chef's Silicone Basting Brush**; sprinkle with ¼ tsp (1 mL) of the black pepper. Arrange bread on **Rectangle Stone**; bake 12-14 minutes or until deep golden brown. Remove baking stone from oven to **Stackable Cooling Rack**.

2 Meanwhile, cut cucumber, onion and jalapeño in half using **Santoku Knife**; set half of each aside. Finely chop plum tomatoes, remaining cucumber, onion and jalapeño; place in **Stainless (4-qt./4-L) Mixing Bowl**. Gently stir in watermelon and ½ cup (125 mL) of the cilantro. Set aside 1 cup (250 mL) of the plum tomato mixture in **(2-cup/500-mL) Prep Bowl**; cover and refrigerate until ready to serve.

3 Cut bell pepper, reserved cucumber and onion into quarters; place into blender container. Add remaining two slices bread, reserved jalapeño, canned tomatoes, vegetable juice, vinegar, pressed garlic, remaining ¼ tsp (1 mL) black pepper and salt to blender; cover and blend until smooth. Pour blended mixture into mixing bowl containing plum tomato mixture; add remaining cilantro and stir gently. Cover and refrigerate 1 hour or until chilled, stirring occasionally.

4 To serve, divide gazpacho evenly among serving bowls. Top with reserved plum tomato mixture and toasted bread.

Cook's Tip

Adding whole grain bread to the soup adds body and additional fiber.

- 1 small poblano pepper
- 1 small red bell pepper
- 1 ear fresh corn, husk and silk removed
- 1 serrano pepper
- 1 lime
- 1 cup (250 mL) diced fresh papaya
- 2 tbsp (30 mL) chopped fresh cilantro
- ¼ tsp (1 mL) salt
- 6 (6-in./15-cm) flour tortillas
- 3 oz (90 g) goat cheese, crumbled
- 4 oz (125 g) grilled chicken breast, thinly sliced (see Cook's Tip)
- Lime wedges (optional)

Nutrition Facts

Serving Size 1 quesadilla, about 1 T salsa
Servings Per Recipe 6

U.S. Nutrients Per Serving

Calories 190	Calories from Fat 50

	% Daily Value
Total Fat 6g	9%
Saturated Fat 2.5g	13%
Trans Fat 0g	
Cholesterol 25mg	8%
Sodium 380mg	16%
Total Carbohydrate 23g	8%
Dietary Fiber 1g	4%
Sugars 3g	
Protein 12g	

U.S. Diabetic Exchanges Per Serving

1½ starch, 1 medium-fat meat (1½ carb)

Chicken & Goat Cheese Quesadillas with Papaya Salsa

Broiling the vegetables gives these quesadillas a bold, slightly smoky flavor.

PREP TIME: 15 MINUTES   **TOTAL TIME:** 40 MINUTES   **YIELD:** 6 SERVINGS

1 Preheat broiler on HIGH. Cut poblano and bell pepper in half lengthwise. Remove and discard stems and seeds. Place corn on **Medium Sheet Pan**. Add poblano and bell pepper, cut sides down. Place pan 2-4 in. (5-10 cm) from heating element. Broil 5-7 minutes or until poblano is charred. Remove pan from broiler. Carefully remove poblano from pan to **Classic Batter Bowl** using **Chef's Tongs**; cover. Turn corn over and return corn and bell pepper to broiler. Broil an additional 10-12 minutes or until corn is lightly browned and bell pepper is soft. Add bell pepper to batter bowl; cover and place in freezer 10 minutes or until completely cooled. Set corn aside to cool.

2 Peel poblano and bell pepper; dice using **Chef's Knife**. Finely chop serrano pepper using **Food Chopper**. Remove corn kernels from cob using **Kernel Cutter**. Juice lime using **Citrus Press** to measure 1 tbsp (15 mL). Combine peppers, corn, juice, papaya, cilantro and salt in **Small Batter Bowl**; mix well. Reserve ½ cup (125 mL) of the salsa.

3 Arrange three of the tortillas on **Double Burner Griddle**. Sprinkle half of the cheese over tortillas. Cook over medium heat 3-5 minutes or until tortillas are lightly browned. Top cheese with half of the chicken and ¼ cup (50 mL) of the salsa. Fold quesadillas in half with **Slotted Turner** and transfer to **Large Grooved Cutting Board**; cut in half. Repeat with remaining tortillas, cheese, chicken and salsa. Serve quesadillas with reserved salsa and lime wedges, if desired.

Cook's Tips

Get ahead by grilling two chicken breasts and saving one for later. Heat **Grill Pan** over medium heat 5 minutes. Sprinkle two 6-oz (175-g) chicken breasts with ⅛ tsp (0.5 mL) *each* salt and coarsely ground black pepper. Place chicken into pan and top with **Grill Press**. Cook 5 minutes on each side or until grill marks appear and internal temperature reaches 165°F (74°C).

To easily peel and chop a papaya, cut it in half lengthwise using **Santoku Knife** and remove seeds. Reserve half for another use. Peel remaining papaya half with **Serrated Peeler**; place cut side down on **Cutting Board**. Slice into ¼-in. (6-mm) slices; dice slices.

MAIN DISHES

- 2 tbsp (30 mL) fresh lemon juice
- 4 tsp (20 mL) **Buffalo Rub**
- 1 tbsp (15 mL) olive oil
- 2 garlic cloves, pressed
- 12 oz (350 g) beef tenderloin filet
- 1/8 tsp (0.5 mL) salt
- 8 jumbo uncooked prawns (10-15 per pound), peeled and deveined
- 1 1/4 lbs (575 g) small Yukon gold potatoes (about 6 potatoes)
- 1 medium red bell pepper
- 2 small red onions
- 1 oz (30 g) blue cheese, crumbled
- 1/4 cup (50 mL) chopped fresh parsley

Nutrition Facts

Serving Size 1 skewer, 5 oz potatoes
Servings Per Recipe 4

U.S. Nutrients Per Serving

Calories 350	Calories from Fat 100

	% Daily Value
Total Fat 11g	**17%**
Saturated Fat 4g	**20%**
Trans Fat 0g	
Cholesterol 135mg	**45%**
Sodium 490mg	**20%**
Total Carbohydrate 31g	**10%**
Dietary Fiber 5g	**20%**
Sugars 6g	
Protein 30g	

U.S. Diabetic Exchanges Per Serving

2 starch, 3 1/2 low-fat meat (2 carb)

Surf & Turf Skewers with Grilled Potato Salad

Lemon juice, garlic and Buffalo Rub make an exciting marinade for this seemingly decadent dish, which is sure to spice up your next barbecue.

PREP TIME: 30 MINUTES   **TOTAL TIME:** 50 MINUTES   **YIELD:** 4 SERVINGS

1 For marinade, combine lemon juice, rub, oil and pressed garlic in **(1-cup/250-mL)
Prep Bowl**; set aside 1 tbsp (15 mL) for later use with skewers. Cut beef into twelve
2-in. (5-cm) pieces. Place beef, half of the remaining marinade and salt into **Classic
Batter Bowl**; mix well. Place prawns and remaining half of the marinade into **Small
Batter Bowl**; mix well. Cover and refrigerate beef and prawns 30 minutes.

2 Meanwhile, cut potatoes into 1/2-inch-thick (1-cm) slices. Place potatoes and 2 cups
(500 mL) water into **Large Micro-Cooker®**. Microwave, covered, on HIGH 14-16 minutes
or until cooked through but still firm; drain. Cut bell pepper into sixteen 1-in. (2.5-cm)
pieces and onions into 16 wedges.

3 Prepare grill for direct cooking over medium-high heat. Alternately thread beef, prawns
and vegetables onto four **BBQ Skewers**. Spray grill with nonstick cooking spray for
grilling. Grill potatoes, uncovered, 2-3 minutes. Turn potatoes over with **BBQ Tongs**;
grill, uncovered, 2-3 minutes or until grill marks appear. Combine potatoes and blue
cheese in **Stainless (4-qt./4-L) Mixing Bowl**; mix well. Set aside and keep warm.

4 Grill skewers, covered, 2-3 minutes or until grill marks appear. Turn over and continue
to grill, covered, 2-3 minutes or until internal temperature of beef reaches 145°F (63°C)
for medium-rare doneness. Brush skewers with reserved marinade. Sprinkle potatoes
with parsley; serve with skewers.

Cook's Tips

To easily turn skewers, slide **BBQ Jumbo Turner** under them and turn skewers using
BBQ Tongs.

If desired, 2 tbsp (30 mL) of cayenne pepper sauce used for making buffalo chicken
wings can be substituted for the Buffalo Rub.

COUSCOUS

- 1½ tsp (7 mL) canola oil
- 1 cup (250 mL) uncooked Israeli couscous
- 1½ tsp (7 mL) curry powder
- 1¼ cups (300 mL) water

CHICKEN & COMPOTE

- 1 tbsp (15 mL) canola oil, divided
- 4 boneless, skinless chicken breasts (3 oz/90 g each)
- ½ tsp (2 mL) salt, divided
- ¼ tsp (1 mL) coarsely ground black pepper
- 2 large shallots, finely chopped
- 1 medium Granny Smith apple, diced
- 1 cup (250 mL) unsalted chicken stock
- ¼ cup (50 mL) dried currants
- 1 tbsp (15 mL) sugar
- 1 tbsp (15 mL) curry powder
- 1½ tsp (7 mL) cornstarch dissolved in ¼ cup (50 mL) cold water
- 1 tbsp (15 mL) light butter
- 3 large fresh apricots, pitted and diced

Nutrition Facts

Serving Size 1 chicken breast,
½ C couscous, ½ C compote
Servings Per Recipe 4

U.S. Nutrients Per Serving

Calories 380	Calories from Fat 80
	% Daily Value
Total Fat 9g	14%
Saturated Fat 2g	10%
Trans Fat 0g	
Cholesterol 50mg	17%
Sodium 400mg	17%
Total Carbohydrate 51g	17%
Dietary Fiber 4g	16%
Sugars 17g	
Protein 24g	

U.S. Diabetic Exchanges Per Serving

2 starch, 1½ fruit, 2½ low-fat meat (3½ carb)

Curry Chicken with Warm Fruit Compote

The aromas, colors and flavors of this Indian-inspired dish are a feast for the senses.

PREP TIME: 15 MINUTES   **TOTAL TIME:** 35 MINUTES   **YIELD:** 4 SERVINGS

1 For couscous, heat oil in **(3-qt./2.8-L) Saucepan** over medium heat 1-3 minutes or until shimmering; add couscous and curry powder. Cook 3-4 minutes or until couscous is golden brown, stirring occasionally. Add water; bring to a boil. Reduce heat to medium-low; cook, covered, 8-10 minutes or until couscous is tender. Remove Saucepan from heat; set aside and keep warm.

2 Meanwhile, for chicken, heat 2 tsp (10 mL) of the oil in **(12-in./30-cm) Skillet** over medium-high heat 1-3 minutes or until shimmering. Flatten chicken to an even thickness with **Meat Tenderizer**; sprinkle with ¼ tsp (1 mL) of the salt and black pepper. Cook chicken 2-2½ minutes on each side or until centers are no longer pink. Remove chicken from Skillet; set aside and keep warm.

3 Add remaining 1 tsp (5 mL) oil, shallots and apple to Skillet; cook and stir 30-60 seconds or until shallots are fragrant. Stir in stock, currants, sugar, curry powder and remaining ¼ tsp (1 mL) salt; cook, uncovered, 1-2 minutes or until mixture comes to a simmer. Slowly add cornstarch mixture to Skillet, stirring constantly; stir in butter. Reduce heat to medium-low. Return chicken to Skillet; cook, covered, 3-4 minutes or until heated through. Stir in apricots. Serve with couscous.

Cook's Tips

To ensure that the cornstarch is fully incorporated, mix the cornstarch mixture again, just before stirring it into Skillet.

If desired, 1 cup (250 mL) (6 oz/175 g) dried apricots cut in half lengthwise can be substituted for the fresh apricots. Add dried apricots in Step 3 with stock and currants; proceed as recipe directs.

8 oz (250 g) uncooked angel hair pasta
1 medium onion
1 large chipotle pepper in adobo sauce
1 tbsp (15 mL) canola oil
4 garlic cloves, pressed
2 tsp (10 mL) chili powder
2 tsp (10 mL) dried oregano
2 pints grape tomatoes
¾ cup (175 mL) unsalted chicken stock
20 fresh mussels, cleaned
   (see Cook's Tip)
2 tbsp (30 mL) salted butter
¼ tsp (1 mL) salt
¾ cup (175 mL) chopped fresh cilantro, divided

Nutrition Facts

Serving Size 5 mussels, 1¼ C pasta
Servings Per Recipe 4

U.S. Nutrients Per Serving

Calories 410	Calories from Fat 120

	% Daily Value
Total Fat 13g	20%
Saturated Fat 4.5g	23%
Trans Fat 0g	
Cholesterol 40mg	13%
Sodium 500mg	21%
Total Carbohydrate 55g	18%
Dietary Fiber 5g	20%
Sugars 7g	
Protein 20g	

U.S. Diabetic Exchanges Per Serving

3 starch, 2 vegetable, 1 medium-fat meat, 1 fat (3 carb)

Spicy Mussels with Angel Hair

Ready in less than 30 minutes, this elegant dish is surprisingly suitable for a busy weeknight dinner.

PREP TIME: 15 MINUTES   **TOTAL TIME:** 25 MINUTES   **YIELD:** 4 SERVINGS

1 Cook pasta according to package directions at the low end of the recommended time, omitting salt and oil. Drain and set aside.

2 Meanwhile, finely chop onion and chipotle pepper using **Food Chopper**. Combine oil, pressed garlic, chili powder and oregano in **(12-in./30-cm) Skillet**. Cook over medium heat 1-2 minutes or until fragrant. Add onion and chipotle pepper; cook 2-3 minutes or until onion is softened. Add tomatoes and stock. Cover and cook 4-6 minutes or until tomatoes begin to soften. Crush tomatoes using **Mix 'N Masher**.

3 Add mussels, butter and salt to Skillet; toss to coat using **Chef's Tongs**. Cover and simmer 2-3 minutes or until mussels are open. (Discard any mussels that do not open.) Remove mussels from Skillet; set aside. Add pasta and ½ cup (125 mL) of the cilantro to Skillet. Cook and stir 1 minute or until pasta is hot.

4 Divide pasta mixture evenly among serving bowls. Top with mussels and sprinkle with remaining cilantro. Serve immediately.

Cook's Tips

To clean mussels, scrub them using a firm brush and rinse well in cold water. Pull out any fibers that extend from within the shells. If any mussels are open, tap them on the counter and wait a few seconds; discard any that do not close.

If desired, 2 pints cherry tomatoes can be substituted for the grape tomatoes.

Ingredients

- 2 cups (500 mL) cooked, mashed sweet potatoes (see Cook's Tip)
- ½ cup (125 mL) part-skim milk ricotta cheese
- 1 large egg
- 1½ cups (375 mL) all-purpose flour, plus additional for dusting
- 6 slices turkey bacon, cut crosswise into ¼-in. (6-mm) strips
- 2 tbsp (30 mL) unsalted butter
- ¼ tsp (1 mL) salt
- ¼ tsp (1 mL) coarsely ground black pepper
- 2 cups (500 mL) unsalted chicken stock
- 1 tbsp (15 mL) chopped fresh sage leaves
- 1 tbsp (15 mL) cornstarch dissolved in 1 tbsp (15 mL) cold water

Nutrition Facts

Serving Size about 14 gnocchi, ⅓ C sauce
Servings Per Recipe 6

U.S. Nutrients Per Serving

Calories 360	Calories from Fat 90	
		% Daily Value
Total Fat 10g		15%
Saturated Fat 5g		25%
Trans Fat 0g		
Cholesterol 70mg		23%
Sodium 490mg		20%
Total Carbohydrate 51g		17%
Dietary Fiber 4g		16%
Sugars 7g		
Protein 14g		

U.S. Diabetic Exchanges Per Serving

3½ starch, ½ medium-fat meat, 1 fat (3½ carb)

Sweet Potato Gnocchi with Bacon & Fresh Sage

The pleasing combination of earthy sage and smoky bacon complements this rustic homemade pasta.

PREP TIME: 30 MINUTES   **TOTAL TIME:** 1 HOUR   **YIELD:** 6 SERVINGS

1 Line **Large Sheet Pan** with **Parchment Paper**; set aside. Combine potatoes, ricotta and egg in **Stainless (4-qt./4-L) Mixing Bowl**. Mix until well blended using **Mix 'N Masher**. Add flour, ½ cup (125 mL) at a time, mixing with gloved hands until a soft dough forms. Transfer dough to well floured **Pastry Mat**; knead 6-8 times or until dough becomes firm, sprinkling with flour as needed. Cut dough into four equal pieces. Roll each piece into a 20-in. (51-cm) log; cut logs into 1-in. (2.5-cm) pieces.

2 Bring 5 qts. (4.75 L) of water to a boil in **(8-qt./7.6-L) Stockpot** over medium-high heat. Meanwhile, cook bacon in **(12-in./30-cm) Skillet** over medium heat 8-10 minutes or until crisp. Remove from Skillet; drain on paper towels.

3 Add gnocchi to Stockpot and immediately stir gently one time. Cook 4-6 minutes or until gnocchi float to the top (do not boil). Transfer gnocchi from Stockpot to sheet pan using **Skimmer**. Melt butter in Skillet over medium heat. Add gnocchi; sprinkle with salt and black pepper. Cook 8-10 minutes or until browned, turning occasionally with **Jumbo Slotted Turner**. Transfer gnocchi to same sheet pan; keep warm.

4 Add stock, sage and bacon to Skillet. Bring to a simmer; whisk in cornstarch mixture using **Silicone Flat Whisk**. Cook 2-3 minutes or until sauce is thickened. Serve gnocchi with sauce.

Cook's Tips

To cook sweet potatoes, cut 2 lbs (1 kg) sweet potatoes in half lengthwise. Place potatoes cut-side down into **Deep Covered Baker** (potatoes will overlap); add ½ cup (125 mL) water. Microwave, covered, on HIGH 10-12 minutes. Carefully remove baker from microwave using **Oven Mitts**. Move center potatoes to ends of baker and outer potatoes to center. Cover; microwave on HIGH 10-12 minutes or until potatoes are easily pierced with a fork. Cool completely and scoop out flesh using **Avocado Peeler**.

Choose turkey bacon that has 65% less fat than regular bacon and contains about 135 mg sodium per slice.

To help prevent cooked gnocchi from sticking together, after removing gnocchi from Stockpot, place onto prepared pan and lightly spray with olive oil using **Kitchen Spritzer**.

Polenta Rounds (see below)

- 1 cup (250 mL) hot water
- 1 oz (30 g) dried porcini mushrooms
- 1½ tsp (7 mL) olive oil
- 2 medium carrots, peeled and finely chopped
- 4 large shallots, finely chopped
- 6 garlic cloves, pressed
- ¼ tsp (1 mL) *each* salt and coarsely ground black pepper
- 1½ tbsp (22 mL) tomato paste
- 1 tbsp (15 mL) finely chopped fresh rosemary leaves
- ½ cup (125 mL) dry red wine such as Cabernet Sauvignon
- 2 medium tomatoes, coarsely chopped
- 1 large zucchini, finely chopped
- 1 can (14.5 oz or 540 mL) no-salt-added cannellini beans, drained and rinsed
- 1 medium yellow bell pepper, finely chopped
- 1¾ oz (50 g) gorgonzola cheese, crumbled

Chopped fresh parsley (optional)

Nutrition Facts

Serving Size about 1⅓ C ragout, 3 polenta rounds
Servings Per Recipe 4

U.S. Nutrients Per Serving

Calories 350	Calories from Fat 70
	% Daily Value
Total Fat 7g	11%
Saturated Fat 3g	15%
Trans Fat 0g	
Cholesterol 10mg	3%
Sodium 490mg	20%
Total Carbohydrate 54g	18%
Dietary Fiber 8g	32%
Sugars 9g	
Protein 14g	

U.S. Diabetic Exchanges Per Serving

3 starch, 2 vegetable, 1 fat (3 carb)

Grilled Polenta with Vegetable Ragout

This vegetable stew makes for a hearty dinner, especially when served over polenta.

PREP TIME: 40 MINUTES   **TOTAL TIME:** 1 HOUR   **YIELD:** 4 SERVINGS

1 Prepare *Polenta Rounds* (see below). Meanwhile, combine water and mushrooms in **(2-cup/500-mL) Prep Bowl**; let stand 8-10 minutes or until mushrooms are softened. Heat oil in **(12-in./30-cm) Skillet** over medium heat 1-3 minutes or until shimmering. Add carrots, shallots, pressed garlic, salt and black pepper to Skillet; cook 6-8 minutes or until carrots are tender, stirring occasionally.

2 Strain mushrooms using **(7-in./18-cm) Strainer** into **Small Batter Bowl**, reserving soaking liquid. Finely chop mushrooms. Add mushrooms, tomato paste and rosemary to Skillet; cook 30-60 seconds, stirring constantly. Stir in wine, tomatoes, zucchini and mushroom soaking liquid; bring to a simmer. Reduce heat to medium-low. Cook, covered, 10 minutes, stirring occasionally. Add beans and bell pepper to Skillet; cook, covered, 2-3 minutes or until beans are heated through.

3 Meanwhile, spray **Grill Pan** with olive oil using **Kitchen Spritzer**; heat pan over medium-high heat 5 minutes. Cook polenta rounds 5-6 minutes on each side or until grill marks appear. Serve ragout over polenta; sprinkle with cheese and chopped parsley, if desired.

POLENTA ROUNDS

- 3¾ cups (925 mL) water
- 1 tbsp (15 mL) finely chopped fresh rosemary leaves
- ¼ tsp (1 mL) coarsely ground black pepper
- ⅛ tsp (0.5 mL) salt
- ¾ cup (175 mL) yellow cornmeal

Bring water, rosemary, black pepper and salt to a boil over medium heat in covered **(4-qt./3.8-L) Casserole**. Slowly add cornmeal, whisking constantly with **Silicone Sauce Whisk** until mixture thickens. Cook, covered, 10 minutes, whisking occasionally. Using **Large Scoop**, scoop polenta evenly into cups of **Muffin Pan**; refrigerate 15-20 minutes or until set. Remove polenta rounds from pan; set aside.

- 2 cups (500 mL) port wine
- 3 tbsp (45 mL) sugar
- 4 4-in. (10-cm) sprigs fresh rosemary, divided
- 18 fresh medium black mission figs
- 4 shallots
- 1¼ lbs (575 g) pork tenderloin
- 2 tsp (10 mL) chopped fresh thyme leaves
- 1 tsp (5 mL) coarsely ground black pepper, divided
- ¾ tsp (4 mL) salt, divided
- 2 tbsp (30 mL) olive oil, divided
- 2 cups (500 mL) unsalted chicken stock
- 1½ tbsp (22 mL) cornstarch dissolved in 2 tbsp (30 mL) cold water
- 1 tbsp (15 mL) salted butter
- 8 oz (250 g) hot cooked broccolini (about 12 spears, see Cook's Tip)

Nutrition Facts

Serving Size 3 medallions, 6 fig halves, ⅓ C sauce, 2 broccolini spears
Servings Per Recipe 6

U.S. Nutrients Per Serving

Calories 470	Calories from Fat 80
	% Daily Value
Total Fat 9g	14%
Saturated Fat 2.5g	13%
Trans Fat 0g	
Cholesterol 65mg	22%
Sodium 420mg	18%
Total Carbohydrate 54g	18%
Dietary Fiber 5g	20%
Sugars 38g	
Protein 25g	

U.S. Diabetic Exchanges Per Serving

½ starch, 3 fruit, 3 low-fat meat (3½ carb)

Herb-Crusted Pork with Figs & Port Wine Sauce

Sweet figs and pork tenderloin encased in fresh rosemary and thyme set the stage for an intimate dinner party.

PREP TIME: 50 MINUTES   **TOTAL TIME:** 50 MINUTES   **YIELD:** 6 SERVINGS

1 Preheat oven to 425°F (220°C). Line **Medium Sheet Pan** with foil; set aside. Combine wine, sugar and 1 sprig of the rosemary in **(2-qt./1.9-L) Saucepan**. Bring to a simmer over medium heat; reduce heat to low and simmer 10 minutes. Cut figs in half lengthwise. Add figs and simmer 10 minutes or until softened. Carefully remove rosemary and figs from Saucepan. Discard rosemary; set figs and wine mixture aside.

2 Meanwhile, thinly slice shallots using **Santoku Knife**; set aside. Finely chop remaining rosemary leaves to measure 2 tsp (10 mL). Trim fat and silver skin from pork. Season pork with finely chopped rosemary, thyme, ½ tsp (2 mL) of the black pepper and ¼ tsp (1 mL) of the salt. Heat 1 tbsp (15 mL) of the oil in **(10-in./24-cm) Skillet** over medium heat 1-3 minutes or until shimmering. Add pork to Skillet; cook 4-5 minutes or until browned on all sides, turning occasionally. Remove Skillet from heat; place pork onto sheet pan. Roast 12-14 minutes or until **Digital Pocket Thermometer** registers 155°F (68°C).

3 Return Skillet to heat. Cook remaining 1 tbsp (15 mL) oil and shallots 20-30 seconds or until fragrant, stirring constantly. Add wine mixture; cook 4-5 minutes or until thick and syrupy. Whisk in stock and cornstarch mixture using **Silicone Flat Whisk**. Simmer 6-8 minutes or until thickened. Remove Skillet from heat; stir in butter and remaining ½ tsp (2 mL) *each* black pepper and salt.

4 Remove pork from oven to **Cutting Board**, tent with foil and let stand 5 minutes (temperature will rise to 160°F/71°C). Slice pork into 1-in. (2.5-cm) medallions; serve with sauce, figs and broccolini.

Cook's Tips

Use the **Skimmer** to easily remove figs from Saucepan. Once figs are removed, use Skimmer to remove fig seeds.

To ensure that the cornstarch is fully incorporated, mix the cornstarch mixture again, just before whisking it into Skillet.

To prepare broccolini, combine 8 oz (250 g) fresh broccolini and ¼ cup (50 mL) water in **Large Micro-Cooker®**. Microwave, covered, on HIGH 2-3 minutes or until crisp-tender; drain.

24	wonton wrappers
½	cup (125 mL) rice vinegar
3	tbsp (45 mL) unsalted creamy peanut butter
3	tbsp (45 mL) reduced-sodium soy sauce
2	tbsp (30 mL) canola oil
2	tsp (10 mL) toasted sesame oil
2	tbsp (30 mL) sugar
2	tsp (10 mL) grated fresh gingerroot
2	garlic cloves, pressed
¼	tsp (1 mL) coarsely ground black pepper

SALAD

3	cups (750 mL) *each* shredded Napa cabbage, red cabbage and Romaine lettuce
4	green onions with tops, thinly sliced
½	tsp (2 mL) canola oil
18	oz (540 g) boneless, skinless chicken breasts
¼	tsp (1 mL) coarsely ground black pepper
⅛	tsp (0.5 mL) salt
3	medium navel oranges, segmented (see Cook's Tip)

Nutrition Facts

Serving Size 2 oz chicken, 1½ C salad
Servings Per Recipe 6

U.S. Nutrients Per Serving

Calories 320	Calories from Fat 90
	% Daily Value
Total Fat 10g	15%
Saturated Fat 1.5g	8%
Trans Fat 0g	
Cholesterol 55mg	18%
Sodium 500mg	21%
Total Carbohydrate 35g	12%
Dietary Fiber 4g	16%
Sugars 11g	
Protein 24g	

U.S. Diabetic Exchanges Per Serving

1 starch, 1 fruit, 1 vegetable,
3 low-fat meat (2 carb)

Crunchy Asian Chicken Salad

Crispy baked wonton strips, a mixture of cabbages and a delicious peanut-soy dressing make this healthy salad surpass restaurant salads.

PREP TIME: 20 MINUTES   **TOTAL TIME:** 35 MINUTES   **YIELD:** 6 SERVINGS

1   Preheat oven to 400°F (200°C). Stack wonton wrappers and cut into eight strips with **Chef's Knife**. Lightly spray strips with nonstick cooking spray; toss to coat. Distribute evenly over **Large Round Stone with Handles**; bake 10-14 minutes or until golden brown. Remove baking stone from oven to **Stackable Cooling Rack**; cool completely.

2   Meanwhile, for dressing, combine vinegar, peanut butter, soy sauce, oils, sugar, ginger, pressed garlic and black pepper in **Small Batter Bowl**; whisk with **Stainless Mini Whisk** until smooth. Set aside. For salad, in **Stainless (6-qt./6-L) Mixing Bowl**, combine cabbages, lettuce and green onions; toss to combine and set aside.

3   Heat oil in **(12-in./30-cm) Skillet** over medium-high heat 1-3 minutes or until shimmering. Cut chicken crosswise into ½-in. (1-cm) slices. Season chicken with black pepper and salt; cook 2-4 minutes or until golden brown, stirring occasionally. Remove chicken from Skillet to **Stainless (2-qt./2-L) Mixing Bowl**; toss with ¼ cup (50 mL) of the dressing.

4   Pour remaining dressing over cabbage mixture; toss gently to coat. Transfer cabbage mixture to **Large Bamboo Square Bowl**, leaving excess dressing in mixing bowl; top with chicken, wonton strips and orange segments.

Cook's Tip

To cut orange into segments, cut a thin slice from the top and the bottom using **Utility Knife**; stand upright. Cutting from top to bottom, carefully trim away peel and white membrane. Cut down one side of membrane. Angle knife under segment and lift out. Repeat with remaining segments.

¼	cup (50 mL) light mayonnaise
1	tsp (5 mL) Dijon mustard
1	tsp (5 mL) fresh lemon juice
½	tsp (2 mL) **Creole Rub**
3	cups (750 mL) fresh corn, divided
⅔	cup (150 mL) all-purpose flour
⅓	cup (75 mL) low-fat buttermilk
¼	cup (50 mL) pasteurized refrigerated egg product
¾	tsp (4 mL) baking powder
2	green onions with tops, thinly sliced
½	tsp (2 mL) coarsely ground black pepper

SHRIMP & SALAD

8	oz (250 g) large uncooked shrimp (21-25 per pound), peeled and deveined
1	tbsp (15 mL) canola oil, divided
2	tsp (10 mL) Creole Rub
1	tsp (5 mL) lemon zest
3½	tbsp (52 mL) fresh lemon juice
6	cups (1.5 L) loosely packed arugula

Nutrition Facts
Serving Size 3 shrimp, 3 cakes,
1½ C salad, 1 T sauce
Servings Per Recipe 4

U.S. Nutrients Per Serving

Calories 340	Calories from Fat 90
	% Daily Value
Total Fat 10g	15%
Saturated Fat 1.5g	8%
Trans Fat 0g	
Cholesterol 90mg	30%
Sodium 500mg	21%
Total Carbohydrate 44g	15%
Dietary Fiber 4g	16%
Sugars 10g	
Protein 21g	

U.S. Diabetic Exchanges Per Serving

2 starch, 1 vegetable, 2 low-fat meat (2 carb)

Sweet Corn Cakes with Creole Shrimp

Homemade corn cakes topped with flavorful shrimp inspire fun times with good friends.

PREP TIME: 30 MINUTES   **TOTAL TIME:** 45 MINUTES   **YIELD:** 4 SERVINGS

1 For sauce, combine mayonnaise, mustard, lemon juice and rub in **(2-cup/500-mL) Prep Bowl**; cover and refrigerate until ready to serve.

2 For cakes, place 1 cup (250 mL) of the corn in **Manual Food Processor**; pump handle until a coarse paste forms. Combine flour, buttermilk, egg product and baking powder in **Classic Batter Bowl**; whisk until smooth. Add corn paste, remaining 2 cups (500 mL) corn, green onions and black pepper to batter bowl; mix well.

3 Lightly spray **Double Burner Griddle** with canola oil using **Kitchen Spritzer**; heat over medium heat 1-3 minutes or until shimmering. Using **Medium Scoop**, scoop corn batter onto Griddle for a total of 12 cakes, lightly pressing down with back of scoop. Cook 4-5 minutes on each side or until cakes are golden brown. Remove cakes from Griddle; keep warm.

4 For shrimp, combine shrimp, 1 tsp (5 mL) of the oil, rub and zest in **Stainless (2-qt./2-L) Mixing Bowl**; toss to coat. Arrange shrimp on Griddle; cook over medium-high heat 1½-2 minutes on each side or until opaque.

5 For salad, whisk together remaining 2 tsp (10 mL) oil and lemon juice in **(1-cup/250-mL) Easy Read Measuring Cup**. Combine arugula and lemon juice mixture in **Stainless (4-qt./4-L) Mixing Bowl**; toss gently. To serve, divide arugula among serving plates; top with corn cakes and shrimp. Drizzle with sauce.

Cook's Tip

If desired, 1¼ tsp (6 mL) paprika, ½ tsp (2 mL) garlic powder and ¼ tsp (1 mL) *each* of salt, cayenne pepper and dried oregano can be substituted for the Creole Rub in the sauce and shrimp. Combine ingredients in **(1-cup/250-mL) Prep Bowl**. Add ½ tsp (2 mL) to sauce and 2 tsp (10 mL) to shrimp.

Chipotle Sauce (see below)

- 2 poblano peppers
- ½ medium red onion
- 1 cup (250 mL) loosely packed fresh cilantro
- 4½ whole wheat hamburger buns, divided
- 2 garlic cloves, pressed
- 1 tsp (5 mL) ground cumin
- ½ tsp (2 mL) coarsely ground black pepper
- ⅛ tsp (0.5 mL) salt
- 1 lb (450 g) 95% lean ground beef

VEGETABLES

- 1½ tsp (7 mL) canola oil, divided
- 12 oz (350 g) Yukon gold potatoes
- 2 poblano peppers
- ½ medium red onion, sliced into quarters
- 1 garlic clove, pressed
- ¼ tsp (1 mL) coarsely ground black pepper
- 1 oz (30 g) queso fresco cheese, crumbled
- ½ cup (125 mL) loosely packed fresh cilantro, snipped

Nutrition Facts

Serving Size 1 burger, ½ C vegetables, ½ T sauce
Servings Per Recipe 4

U.S. Nutrients Per Serving

Calories 440	Calories from Fat 110
	% Daily Value
Total Fat 13g	20%
Saturated Fat 3.5g	18%
Trans Fat 0g	
Cholesterol 75mg	25%
Sodium 470mg	20%
Total Carbohydrate 50g	17%
Dietary Fiber 8g	32%
Sugars 6g	
Protein 33g	

U.S. Diabetic Exchanges Per Serving

3 starch, 3½ low-fat meat (3 carb)

Spicy Poblano Burgers

Yes, beef burgers can be healthy! Poblano peppers and cilantro zest them up, and the roasted vegetables stand in for fries.

PREP TIME: 15 MINUTES   **TOTAL TIME:** 45 MINUTES   **YIELD:** 4 SERVINGS

1 Prepare *Chipotle Sauce* (see below). Preheat broiler on HIGH. For burgers, place poblanos on **Large Sheet Pan**. Place pan 2-4 in. (5-10 cm) from heating element. Broil poblanos 8 minutes, carefully turning after 6 minutes. Place in large resealable plastic bag 15 minutes. *Reduce oven temperature to 450°F (230°C).*

2 For vegetables, brush same sheet pan with ½ tsp (2 mL) of the oil; set aside. Cut potatoes into ½-in. (1-cm) slices; cut slices into ½-in. (1-cm) strips. Cut poblanos in half lengthwise and onion into quarters. Combine potatoes, poblanos, onion, pressed garlic, black pepper and remaining 1 tsp (5 mL) oil in **Classic Batter Bowl**; mix well. Spread vegetables evenly over pan; roast 30-35 minutes or until potatoes are tender, stirring occasionally. Remove pan from oven to **Stackable Cooling Rack**. Cool slightly; cut poblanos into strips.

3 Meanwhile, remove skin and seeds from broiled poblanos. Finely chop poblanos, onion and cilantro with **Food Chopper**. Tear half of a hamburger bun into pieces. Place poblanos, onion, cilantro, hamburger bun pieces, pressed garlic, cumin, black pepper and salt in **Stainless (4-qt./4-L) Mixing Bowl**; mix pieces until a smooth paste forms. Add beef; mix gently until incorporated. Form beef mixture into four ¾-inch-thick (2-cm) patties.

4 Preheat **Grill Pan** and **Grill Press** over medium-high heat 5 minutes. Place patties in pan; top with press and cook 3-4 minutes on each side or until grill marks appear and internal temperature reaches 160°F (71°C). Transfer burgers to paper towel-lined plate; let stand 5 minutes. Place burgers on bun bottoms, top with *Chipotle Sauce*. Serve burgers with vegetables; sprinkle vegetables with cheese and cilantro.

CHIPOTLE SAUCE

- 2 tbsp (30 mL) light mayonnaise
- 1 tsp (5 mL) lime juice
- ½ tsp (2 mL) adobo sauce (from can of chipotle peppers in adobo sauce)

Combine all ingredients in **(1-cup/250-mL) Prep Bowl**; mix well. Cover and refrigerate until ready to serve.

1	lime
3	cups (750 mL) loosely packed fresh cilantro
1½	cups (375 mL) loosely packed fresh basil leaves
2	green onions with tops, cut into thirds
3	tbsp (45 mL) water
1	garlic clove, peeled
½	tsp (2 mL) grated fresh gingerroot
½	tsp (2 mL) crushed red pepper flakes
¼	tsp (1 mL) salt

CHICKEN & RICE

18	low-sodium butter-flavored crackers, crushed
4	boneless, skinless chicken breasts (3 oz/90 g each)
2	tbsp (30 mL) light mayonnaise
¼	tsp (1 mL) *each* salt and coarsely ground black pepper
1	tbsp (15 mL) canola oil
1½	cups (375 mL) hot cooked sushi rice (see Cook's Tip)

Chicken with Fresh Herb Chimichurri

This crisp breaded and pan-fried chicken is topped with an Asian-inspired herb mixture that explodes with fresh flavors.

PREP TIME: 20 MINUTES   **TOTAL TIME:** 35 MINUTES   **YIELD:** 4 SERVINGS

1 For chimichurri, using **Citrus Press**, juice lime to measure 1 tbsp (15 mL). Place juice, cilantro, basil, green onions, water, garlic and ginger in **Manual Food Processor**. Cover and pump handle until coarsely pureed. Pour chimichuri into **Small Batter Bowl**. Stir in red pepper flakes and salt. Set chimichurri aside.

2 For chicken, place cracker crumbs into **Coating Tray**; microwave on HIGH 2-3 minutes or until deep golden brown, stirring every 30 seconds. Flatten chicken to a ½-in. (1-cm) thickness with **Meat Tenderizer**. Brush chicken with mayonnaise using **Chef's Silicone Basting Brush**; season with salt and black pepper. Dredge chicken in cracker crumbs, firmly pressing to coat.

3 Heat oil in **Executive (12-in./30-cm) Skillet** (do not use stainless cookware) over medium heat 1-3 minutes or until shimmering. Cook chicken 3-4 minutes on each side or until centers are no longer pink. Place rice and 3 tbsp (45 mL) of the chimichurri into **Classic Batter Bowl**; mix well. Serve chicken with rice and remaining chimichurri.

Cook's Tips

Chimichurri is a thick herb sauce that is popular in Argentina.

Sushi rice is a short grain rice widely used in Asian cooking and can be found in the ethnic section of most grocery stores.

Nutrition Facts

Serving Size 1 chicken breast, about ⅓ C rice, ¼ C chimichurri
Servings Per Recipe 4

U.S. Nutrients Per Serving

Calories 360	Calories from Fat 100

	% Daily Value
Total Fat 11g	**17%**
Saturated Fat 2g	**10%**
Trans Fat 0g	
Cholesterol 50mg	**17%**
Sodium 430mg	**18%**
Total Carbohydrate 41g	**14%**
Dietary Fiber 2g	**8%**
Sugars 1g	
Protein 21g	

U.S. Diabetic Exchanges Per Serving

2½ starch, 1 vegetable, 2 low-fat meat (2½ carb)

Ingredients

- ½ cup (125 mL) uncooked whole wheat couscous
- 1 lemon, divided
- 1 container (6 oz) plain nonfat Greek yogurt (⅔ cup/150 mL)
- 4 oz (125 g) fat-free feta cheese, crumbled, divided
- ½ cup (125 mL) loosely packed fresh mint leaves, finely chopped, divided
- 2 garlic cloves, pressed, divided
- 1¼ tsp (6 mL) coarsely ground black pepper, divided
- 1 cup (250 mL) grape tomatoes
- ½ medium red onion
- 1 can (14.5 oz/540 mL) garbanzo beans, drained and rinsed
- 1 tbsp (15 mL) olive oil
- 1 lb (450 g) turkey breast cutlets, sliced into 2-in. (5-cm) strips
- ¼ tsp (1 mL) salt
- 1 tbsp (15 mL) fresh oregano leaves, finely chopped
- 12 large Boston lettuce leaves

Nutrition Facts

Serving Size 2 wraps
Servings Per Recipe 6

U.S. Nutrients Per Serving

Calories 230	Calories from Fat 30

	% Daily Value
Total Fat 3.5g	5%
Saturated Fat 0g	0%
Trans Fat 0g	
Cholesterol 35mg	12%
Sodium 450mg	19%
Total Carbohydrate 19g	6%
Dietary Fiber 4g	16%
Sugars 3g	
Protein 30g	

U.S. Diabetic Exchanges Per Serving

1 starch, 1 vegetable, 3½ low-fat meat (1 carb)

Mediterranean Lettuce Wraps

These lettuce wraps are a fun and unique way to serve this turkey and couscous salad.

PREP TIME: 25 MINUTES   **TOTAL TIME:** 30 MINUTES   **YIELD:** 6 SERVINGS

1 Prepare couscous according to package directions, using water instead of broth and omitting salt and oil; set aside and keep warm. Meanwhile, for sauce, juice lemon using **Juicer** to measure 2 tbsp (30 mL). Set aside 1 tbsp (15 mL) for use in salad. Using **Small Mix 'N Scraper®**, mix remaining 1 tbsp (15 mL) juice, yogurt, half of the cheese, half of the mint, one of the pressed garlic cloves and ¼ tsp (1 mL) of the black pepper in **(2-cup/500-mL) Prep Bowl**; set aside.

2 For salad, cut tomatoes lengthwise into quarters and thinly slice onion lengthwise using **Chef's Knife**. Combine tomatoes, onion, beans, reserved lemon juice, remaining mint, remaining pressed garlic clove and ¼ tsp (1 mL) of the black pepper in **Classic Batter Bowl**; toss gently with **Mix 'N Scraper®** and set aside.

3 For filling, add oil to **(12-in./30-cm) Skillet**; heat over medium-high heat 1-3 minutes or until shimmering. Place turkey, salt and remaining ¾ tsp (4 mL) black pepper in **Stainless (4-qt./4-L) Mixing Bowl**; toss to coat. Cook turkey, uncovered, 2-3 minutes or until golden brown, stirring occasionally. Remove Skillet from heat. Add couscous, remaining cheese and oregano; stir until combined.

4 To serve, spoon filling onto lettuce leaves; top with salad and drizzle with sauce.

Cook's Tips

Turkey cutlets are thinly sliced boneless, skinless turkey breasts.

Boston lettuce is a leafy lettuce with soft leaves and a buttery texture and flavor. If desired, Bibb or iceberg lettuce can be substituted.

- 6 oz (175 g) uncooked straight-cut rice noodles (see Cook's Tip)
- 2 tbsp (30 mL) reduced-sodium soy sauce
- 1 tsp (5 mL) grated fresh gingerroot
- 1 pkg (14 oz or 397 g) extra-firm tofu, drained
- 1 tsp (5 mL) canola oil

SAUCE & STIR-FRY

- ¼ cup (50 mL) no-salt-added ketchup
- ¼ cup (50 mL) rice vinegar
- 3 tbsp (45 mL) packed brown sugar
- 2 tsp (10 mL) toasted sesame oil
- 1 tsp (5 mL) grated fresh gingerroot
- ¼ tsp (1 mL) salt
- 1 medium red bell pepper
- 1 cup (250 mL) fresh snow peas, trimmed
- ½ tsp (2 mL) canola oil
- ¼ cup (50 mL) unsalted chicken stock
- 4 oz (125 g) fresh pineapple, cut into 1-in. (2.5-cm) pieces

  Chopped green onions (optional)

Nutrition Facts

Serving Size 1 piece tofu, about 1 C noodles
Servings Per Recipe 4

U.S. Nutrients Per Serving

Calories 400	Calories from Fat 90

	% Daily Value
Total Fat 10g	15%
Saturated Fat 1.5g	8%
Trans Fat 0g	
Cholesterol 0mg	0%
Sodium 400mg	17%
Total Carbohydrate 60g	20%
Dietary Fiber 4g	16%
Sugars 19g	
Protein 16g	

U.S. Diabetic Exchanges Per Serving

2 starch, 2 fruit, 1½ low-fat meat, 1 fat (4 carb)

Pan-Roasted Tofu with Sweet & Sour Noodles

Marinating tofu in ginger and soy sauce gives this meatless main dish an extra punch of flavor.

PREP TIME: 20 MINUTES   **TOTAL TIME:** 35 MINUTES   **YIELD:** 4 SERVINGS

1 Soak noodles according to package directions for stir-fry. Drain and set aside. Meanwhile, for tofu, combine soy sauce and ginger in **(1-cup/250-mL) Prep Bowl**. Cut tofu in half lengthwise. Cut each half diagonally for a total of four triangles. Combine soy sauce mixture and tofu in a large resealable plastic bag. Seal bag and turn carefully to coat; refrigerate 20 minutes.

2 For sauce, combine ketchup, vinegar, brown sugar, sesame oil, ginger and salt in **(2-cup/500-mL) Prep Bowl**; whisk well using **Stainless Mini Whisk** and set aside. Slice bell pepper into thin strips. Cut peas on a bias into 1-in. (2.5-cm) pieces.

3 Remove tofu from marinade; discard marinade. Heat canola oil in **(12-in./30-cm) Skillet** over medium-high heat 1-3 minutes or until shimmering. Add tofu to Skillet. Cook 1½-2½ minutes on each side or until golden brown. Remove tofu from Skillet; tent with foil to keep warm.

4 For stir-fry, return Skillet to heat. Add canola oil and bell pepper to Skillet. Cook 1-2 minutes or until crisp-tender. Add noodles, stock and sauce. Cook 2-4 minutes or until noodles are softened, tossing often using **Chef's Tongs**. Stir in peas and pineapple. Cook 1-2 minutes or until peas are crisp-tender. Serve stir-fry with tofu; sprinkle with chopped green onions, if desired.

Cook's Tip

Use rice noodles labeled "straight cut" or other thicker-cut rice noodles recommended for stir-fry.

1 small shallot

1 orange

2 tbsp (30 mL) chopped fresh tarragon leaves, divided

1 tbsp (15 mL) Dijon mustard

1 tbsp (15 mL) white wine vinegar

½ tsp (2 mL) coarsely ground black pepper, divided

¼ tsp (1 mL) plus ⅛ tsp (0.5 mL) salt, divided

2 tbsp (30 mL) canola oil

1 medium red bell pepper, roasted (see Cook's Tip)

1 cup (250 mL) unsalted chicken stock

¾ cup (175 mL) uncooked couscous

16 large sea scallops (see Cook's Tip)

Nutrition Facts

Serving Size 4 scallops, ½ C couscous, about 1 T vinaigrette
Servings Per Recipe 4

U.S. Nutrients Per Serving

Calories 270	Calories from Fat 70

	% Daily Value
Total Fat 8g	**12%**
Saturated Fat 0.5g	**3%**
Trans Fat 0g	
Cholesterol 20mg	**7%**
Sodium 450mg	**19%**
Total Carbohydrate 32g	**11%**
Dietary Fiber 2g	**8%**
Sugars 2g	
Protein 16g	

U.S. Diabetic Exchanges Per Serving

2 starch, 2 low-fat meat (2 carb)

Grilled Sea Scallops with Roasted Red Pepper Couscous

Delicate scallops rest on a bed of colorful couscous and are drizzled with homemade Dijon-orange vinaigrette for an artistic presentation.

PREP TIME: 20 MINUTES   **TOTAL TIME:** 35 MINUTES   **YIELD:** 4 SERVINGS

1 For vinaigrette, finely chop shallot. Juice orange using **Juicer** to measure 2 tbsp (30 mL). Combine shallot, juice, 1 tbsp (15 mL) of the tarragon, mustard, vinegar and ¼ tsp (1 mL) *each* of the black pepper and salt in **Small Batter Bowl**; whisk well. Slowly add oil, whisking until well blended. Set aside.

2 Slice roasted bell pepper into 1-in. (2.5-cm) strips using **Chef's Knife**. Microwave stock in **Large Micro-Cooker®** on HIGH 2-3 minutes or until simmering. Add couscous; cover and let stand 5 minutes. Add roasted bell pepper and remaining 1 tbsp (15 mL) tarragon; mix well using **Classic Scraper**. Set aside and keep warm.

3 Meanwhile, pat scallops dry using paper towels. Season scallops with remaining ¼ tsp (1 mL) black pepper and ⅛ tsp (0.5 mL) salt. Heat **Grill Pan** over medium-high heat 5 minutes. Lightly spray pan with canola oil using **Kitchen Spritzer**. Cook scallops 2-3 minutes on each side or until grill marks appear.

4 Divide couscous among serving plates; top with scallops and drizzle with vinaigrette.

Cook's Tips

To roast red bell pepper, place directly over gas flame on high heat or under broiler. Cook 8-10 minutes or until charred on all sides, carefully turning occasionally using **Chef's Tongs**. Carefully remove from heat or broiler and place in large resealable plastic bag. Seal bag and refrigerate 10 minutes or until cooled; remove and discard skin, seeds and stem.

Sea scallops have a small fibrous muscle on the side which should be removed because it can toughen when cooked.

Patting scallops dry with paper towels ensures the best browning when grilled.

2	tbsp (30 mL) Dijon mustard
2	tbsp (30 mL) red wine vinegar
1	tbsp (15 mL) honey
1	small shallot, finely chopped
1	tsp (5 mL) chopped fresh thyme leaves
⅛	tsp (0.5 mL) salt
1½	tbsp (22 mL) olive oil

SALAD & STEAK

1¼	lbs (575 g) petite golden or fingerling potatoes
1	cup (250 mL) cherry tomatoes
2	small shallots
1	bunch fresh watercress (6 cups/1.5 L)
1¼	lbs (575 g) boneless beef top sirloin steak, about ½ in. (1 cm) thick
1	tsp (5 mL) chopped fresh thyme leaves
1	tsp (5 mL) coarsely ground black pepper
¼	tsp (1 mL) salt

Nutrition Facts

Serving Size 2 oz steak, 1⅓ C salad
Servings Per Recipe 6

U.S. Nutrients Per Serving

Calories 240	Calories from Fat 60
	% Daily Value
Total Fat 7g	11%
Saturated Fat 2g	10%
Trans Fat 0g	
Cholesterol 35mg	12%
Sodium 320mg	13%
Total Carbohydrate 22g	7%
Dietary Fiber 2g	8%
Sugars 5g	
Protein 21g	

U.S. Diabetic Exchanges Per Serving

1 starch, 1 vegetable, 2½ low-fat meat (1 carb)

Warm "Meat & Potato" Salad

Peppery watercress, grilled steak and creamy potatoes are drizzled with a tangy vinaigrette for a healthy, flavorful salad.

PREP TIME: 30 MINUTES   **TOTAL TIME:** 50 MINUTES   **YIELD:** 6 SERVINGS

1   For vinaigrette, combine mustard, vinegar, honey, shallot, thyme and salt in **Small Batter Bowl**. Slowly add oil, whisking until well blended. Set aside.

2   For salad, slice potatoes crosswise into ¼-inch-thick (6-mm) pieces. Combine potatoes and 5 cups (1.2 L) water in **(4-qt./3.8-L) Casserole**; cook over medium heat 13-15 minutes or until tender. Drain and set aside. Cut tomatoes into quarters and thinly slice shallots using **Santoku Knife**. Wash watercress in **Salad & Berry Spinner**; spin dry.

3   Sprinkle both sides of steak with thyme, black pepper and salt. Heat **Grill Pan** over medium-high heat 5 minutes. Spray pan with olive oil using **Kitchen Spritzer**. Add steak to pan and top with **Grill Press**. Cook 2-3 minutes on each side or until **Digital Pocket Thermometer** registers 140°F (60°C) for medium-rare doneness. Remove steak from heat; tent with foil and let stand 5 minutes (temperature will rise to 145°F/63°C).

4   To assemble, combine potatoes, shallots and half of the vinaigrette in medium **Colander Bowl**; toss gently. Thinly slice steak against the grain. Arrange watercress on **Large Bamboo Platter**. Top with potato mixture, tomatoes and steak. Drizzle with remaining vinaigrette.

Cook's Tips

If desired, 1 tsp (5 mL) dried thyme (½ tsp/2 mL in vinaigrette, ½ tsp/2 mL on steak) can be substituted for the fresh thyme.

Watercress has small, dark green leaves and is typically sold in bunches in the produce section of most grocery stores. It has a slightly bitter, peppery taste.

If desired, 1 cup (250 mL) grape tomatoes can be substituted for the cherry tomatoes.

- ⅔ cup (150 mL) apricot fruit spread (see Cook's Tip)
- 1 tbsp (15 mL) wasabi paste (see Cook's Tip)
- ½ cup (125 mL) rice vinegar
- 2 tbsp (30 mL) canola oil
- 2 tsp (10 mL) toasted sesame oil
- 2½ tbsp (37 mL) reduced-sodium soy sauce
- 1 garlic clove, pressed
- 4 oz (125 g) rice noodles or vermicelli (see Cook's Tip)
- 2 cups (500 mL) small broccoli florets
- 4 skinless Ahi (yellowfin) tuna steaks (4 oz/125 g each)
- ¼ tsp (1 mL) coarsely ground black pepper
- 1 medium red bell pepper, thinly sliced
- 2 green onions with tops, thinly sliced

Nutrition Facts

Serving Size 1 tuna steak, 1 C salad
Servings Per Recipe 4

U.S. Nutrients Per Serving

Calories 450	Calories from Fat 100

	% Daily Value
Total Fat 11g	17%
Saturated Fat 1g	5%
Trans Fat 0g	
Cholesterol 50mg	17%
Sodium 490mg	20%
Total Carbohydrate 56g	19%
Dietary Fiber 2g	8%
Sugars 1g	
Protein 31g	

U.S. Diabetic Exchanges Per Serving

1 starch, 2 fruit, 2 vegetable, 3 medium-fat meat (3 carb)

Wasabi-Glazed Ahi Tuna with Rice Noodle Salad

The spicy Asian flavors of the glaze and dressing pair well with the tuna and noodle salad.

PREP TIME: 35 MINUTES   **TOTAL TIME:** 40 MINUTES   **YIELD:** 4 SERVINGS

1   Place fruit spread and wasabi paste in **Small Batter Bowl**; mix until well blended. Set aside ⅓ cup (75 mL) of the wasabi glaze in **(1-cup/250-mL) Prep Bowl** for later use. For dressing, add vinegar, oils, soy sauce and pressed garlic to batter bowl. Whisk until well blended; set aside.

2   For noodle salad, microwave 6 cups (1.5 L) water in **Classic Batter Bowl** on HIGH 5-7 minutes or until hot. Stir in noodles and broccoli; cover and let stand 10-12 minutes or until noodles are softened. Drain noodles and broccoli with medium **Stainless Mesh Colander**. Cool 5 minutes. Return to batter bowl; set aside to cool completely.

3   Heat **Grill Pan** over medium-high heat 5 minutes. Using **Chef's Silicone Basting Brush**, brush tops of tuna with 2 tbsp (30 mL) of the reserved glaze. Grill tuna, glaze side down, 1 minute. Brush tuna with remaining glaze. Turn tuna over and grill 1 minute or until grill marks appear. (Interior of tuna will be rare. *Do not overcook.*) Remove tuna from pan; sprinkle with black pepper.

4   Add bell pepper, onions and dressing to noodles; toss gently to coat. Serve tuna with noodle salad.

Cook's Tips

Choose a fruit spread that is sweetened with fruit syrup from apple, pineapple or pear juice concentrate.

Wasabi paste (Japanese horseradish) is an essential condiment in Japanese cuisine. It is a bright green paste that accompanies sushi, seafood and noodles. Wasabi paste comes packaged in a tube and can be found in the Asian section of most grocery stores.

Rice noodles or vermicelli are used throughout Asian cooking in soups, spring rolls, cold salads and stir-fries. They are similar to bean threads, only longer and made with rice flour instead of mung bean starch. They can be located in the Asian section of most grocery stores.

Ahi tuna has bright red flesh. When purchasing ahi tuna, look for solid, firm flesh with a rosy cast and no "off" odors. For best flavor and texture, serve ahi tuna rare.

- 1 tbsp (15 mL) canola oil, divided
- ¾ cup (175 mL) uncooked bulghur wheat
- 3-4 limes
- 1 small chipotle pepper in adobo sauce plus 1 tbsp (15 mL) adobo sauce, divided
- 1 garlic clove, pressed
- 12 oz (350 g) boneless, skinless chicken breasts
- 2 plum tomatoes, seeded
- ½ cup (125 mL) canned black beans, drained and rinsed
- ½ cup (125 mL) chopped fresh cilantro
- ⅓ cup (75 mL) chopped red onion
- 4 (11-in./28-cm) low-fat, low-sodium flour tortillas, warmed (see Cook's Tip)

  Salsa, fat-free sour cream and lime wedges (optional)

Nutrition Facts

Serving Size 1 burrito
Servings Per Recipe 4

U.S. Nutrients Per Serving

Calories 410	Calories from Fat 70

	% Daily Value
Total Fat 8g	12%
Saturated Fat 2g	10%
Trans Fat 0g	
Cholesterol 45mg	15%
Sodium 360mg	15%
Total Carbohydrate 62g	21%
Dietary Fiber 13g	52%
Sugars 2g	
Protein 28g	

U.S. Diabetic Exchanges Per Serving

4 starch, 2 low-fat meat (4 carb)

Southwestern Tabbouleh Burritos

Bulghur wheat is the base for tabbouleh, which gets a zesty Southwestern flair when wrapped in tortillas with chicken and beans.

PREP TIME: 25 MINUTES   **TOTAL TIME:** 50 MINUTES   **YIELD:** 4 SERVINGS

1. In **(3-qt./2.8-L) Saucepan**, bring 1 cup (250 mL) water and 1 tsp (5 mL) of the oil to a boil; stir in bulghur. Cover and remove from heat; let stand 25 minutes or until water is absorbed.

2. Meanwhile, for marinade, zest lime using **Microplane® Adjustable Fine Grater** to measure 1 tbsp (15 mL). Juice limes using **Citrus Press** to measure ⅓ cup (75 mL). Combine zest, juice, adobo sauce, pressed garlic and remaining 2 tsp (10 mL) oil in **(2-cup/500-mL) Prep Bowl**; mix well. Reserve ¼ cup (50 mL) of the marinade for tabbouleh. Place chicken and remaining marinade in large resealable plastic bag; turn to coat. Refrigerate 20 minutes.

3. For tabbouleh, dice tomatoes and finely chop chipotle pepper to measure 1½ tsp (7 mL) with **Santoku Knife**. Combine bulghur, tomatoes, chipotle pepper, beans, cilantro, onion and reserved marinade in **Classic Batter Bowl**; mix well.

4. Heat **Grill Pan** over medium heat 5 minutes. Remove chicken from marinade; discard marinade. Cook chicken 5 minutes on each side or until internal temperature reaches 165°F (74°C) in thickest part of chicken and center is no longer pink. Thinly slice chicken crosswise. Add chicken to tabbouleh; mix well.

5. Spoon tabbouleh evenly down centers of tortillas. Fold in ends of tortillas and roll up tightly. Cut burritos diagonally in half. Serve with salsa, sour cream and lime wedges, if desired.

Cook's Tips

Bulghur wheat is made from whole grain wheat. It is low in fat and has a mild nutty flavor.

Warming tortillas will make them easier to roll up. To warm tortillas, place them between paper towels. Microwave on HIGH 30-45 seconds or until warm.

- ½ cup (125 mL) white balsamic vinegar
- 3 tbsp (45 mL) packed brown sugar
- 2 tsp (10 mL) Dijon mustard
- 1 tsp (5 mL) olive oil
- ¼ tsp (1 mL) salt
- ¼ tsp (1 mL) coarsely ground black pepper

SALAD & CHICKEN

- 1¼ cups (300 mL) uncooked wild rice blend (see Cook's Tip)
- 1 medium pear
- 2 green onions with tops
- 1 cup (250 mL) seedless red grapes
- ⅓ cup (75 mL) coarsely chopped hazelnuts, toasted
- 18 oz (540 g) boneless, skinless chicken breasts
- ¼ tsp (1 mL) *each* salt and coarsely ground black pepper
- 12 green leaf lettuce leaves
- 2 oz (60 g) blue cheese, crumbled

Nutrition Facts

Serving Size 2 oz chicken, 1¼ C salad
Servings Per Recipe 6

U.S. Nutrients Per Serving

Calories 410	Calories from Fat 100
	% Daily Value
Total Fat 12g	18%
Saturated Fat 2.5g	13%
Trans Fat 0g	
Cholesterol 60mg	20%
Sodium 480mg	20%
Total Carbohydrate 55g	18%
Dietary Fiber 5g	20%
Sugars 20g	
Protein 25g	

U.S. Diabetic Exchanges Per Serving

3 starch, ½ fruit, 2 medium-fat meat
(3½ carb)

Autumn Wild Rice Salad with Chicken

This chicken and wild rice salad also features vegetables, fruits and nuts for a satisfying main dish.

PREP TIME: 15 MINUTES   **TOTAL TIME:** 1 HOUR   **YIELD:** 6 SERVINGS

1 For dressing, whisk together ingredients in **(1-cup/250-mL) Easy Read Measuring Cup**; set aside.

2 For salad, prepare rice blend according to package directions, omitting salt and oil. Place cooked rice in **Stainless (4-qt./4-L) Mixing Bowl**; set aside to cool. Meanwhile, thinly slice pear and onions. Cut pear slices and grapes in half. Add pear, onions, grapes and hazelnuts to mixing bowl. Pour dressing over rice mixture; mix gently with **Mix 'N Scraper®** until well coated.

3 Spray **(12-in./30-cm) Skillet** with canola oil using **Kitchen Spritzer**; heat over medium-high heat 1-3 minutes or until shimmering. Flatten chicken to an even thickness using **Meat Tenderizer**; season with salt and black pepper. Cook chicken 3-4 minutes on each side or until centers are no longer pink. Remove chicken from Skillet to **Cutting Board**; set aside to cool. Thinly slice chicken.

4 To serve, divide lettuce leaves among serving plates; top with rice mixture, chicken and cheese.

Cook's Tips

Packaged wild rice blend consists of a variety of wild rice and whole grain brown rice and can be found with other rice varieties in most grocery stores.

To toast hazelnuts, place whole hazelnuts in **Small Micro-Cooker®**; microwave, covered, on HIGH 2-4 minutes or until toasted, stirring every 30 seconds.

- 2 large leeks, white and light green parts only
- 1 tbsp (15 mL) salted butter
- 1 medium onion, finely chopped
- 3 garlic cloves, pressed
- 1½ tsp (7 mL) smoked paprika
- 2 lbs (1 kg) Yukon gold potatoes, peeled and diced (see Cook's Tip)
- 4 cups (1 L) unsalted chicken stock
- 1 can (14.5 oz or 398 mL) no-salt-added Great Northern beans, drained and rinsed
- 1½ cups (375 mL) 2% milk
- 3 oz (90 g) extra sharp white cheddar cheese, shredded
- ½ tsp (2 mL) salt
- ½ tsp (2 mL) coarsely ground black pepper
- 6 tbsp (90 mL) reduced-fat sour cream
- Snipped fresh chives and additional smoked paprika (optional)

Smoky Yukon Gold Potato Chowder

Smooth and buttery, this potato-and-bean chowder will warm you up.

PREP TIME: 40 MINUTES   **TOTAL TIME:** 45 MINUTES   **YIELD:** 6 SERVINGS

1 Cut leeks in half lengthwise; thinly slice crosswise. Place into **Stainless (4-qt./4-L) Mixing Bowl** and swish in cold water to remove dirt. Drain leeks using medium **Stainless Mesh Colander**.

2 Melt butter in **(8-qt./7.6-L) Stockpot** over medium heat. Add leeks, onion, pressed garlic and paprika to Stockpot; cook, uncovered, 3-4 minutes or until vegetables are softened, stirring occasionally. Add potatoes; cook 2 minutes, stirring constantly. Add stock; cook, covered, 12-15 minutes or until potatoes are fork-tender, stirring occasionally. Add beans; cook 1-2 minutes or until heated through. Remove Stockpot from heat; cool 5 minutes.

3 Carefully ladle one-third of the potato mixture into blender container. Cover and blend until smooth. Pour blended potato mixture into **Stainless (6-qt./6-L) Mixing Bowl**. Repeat with remaining potato mixture.

4 Return blended potato mixture to Stockpot; stir in milk. Cook, uncovered, over medium heat 2-3 minutes or until simmering. Stir in cheese, salt and black pepper. Cook 2-3 minutes or until cheese is melted. Garnish each serving with sour cream, chives and additional paprika, if desired.

Cook's Tip

Yukon gold potatoes have a skin and flesh that ranges from buttery yellow to golden in color. These boiling potatoes have a moist and succulent texture and are suited for baking, mashing and roasting.

Nutrition Facts

Serving Size 1½ C soup, 1 T sour cream
Servings Per Recipe 6

U.S. Nutrients Per Serving

Calories 320	Calories from Fat 90
	% Daily Value
Total Fat 10g	15%
Saturated Fat 6g	30%
Trans Fat 0g	
Cholesterol 35mg	12%
Sodium 460mg	19%
Total Carbohydrate 45g	15%
Dietary Fiber 6g	24%
Sugars 7g	
Protein 15g	

U.S. Diabetic Exchanges Per Serving

3 starch, 1 medium-fat meat (3 carb)

MARINADE & FISH

2 tbsp (30 mL) reduced-sodium
soy sauce

1 tbsp (15 mL) grated fresh gingerroot

1 tsp (5 mL) toasted sesame oil

1 tsp (5 mL) sugar

1 garlic clove, pressed

4 skinless halibut fillets
(4 oz/125 g each), ¾ in. (2 cm) thick

BROTH & NOODLES

2 cups (500 mL) snow peas, trimmed

3 green onions with tops, divided

6 oz (175 g) fresh shiitake mushroom
caps

1 1-in. (2.5-cm) piece peeled
fresh gingerroot

1 tsp (5 mL) canola oil

1 garlic clove, pressed

4 cups (1 L) unsalted chicken stock

8 oz (250 g) uncooked soba noodles

2 tbsp (30 mL) mirin (see Cook's Tip)

1 tbsp (15 mL) reduced-sodium
soy sauce

1 tsp (5 mL) sugar

Nutrition Facts

Serving Size 1 fillet, 1¼ C broth and noodles
Servings Per Recipe 4

U.S. Nutrients Per Serving

Calories 420	Calories from Fat 50

	% Daily Value
Total Fat 5g	8%
Saturated Fat 0.5g	3%
Trans Fat 0g	
Cholesterol 35mg	12%
Sodium 460mg	19%
Total Carbohydrate 55g	18%
Dietary Fiber 5g	20%
Sugars 7g	
Protein 37g	

U.S. Diabetic Exchanges Per Serving

3 starch, 2 vegetable, 3½ meat (3 carb)

Grilled Halibut with Soba Noodles in Asian Broth

This Japanese-inspired noodle dish starts with halibut in a soy-ginger marinade.

PREP TIME: 30 MINUTES   **TOTAL TIME:** 40 MINUTES   **YIELD:** 4 SERVINGS

1 For marinade, in **(2-cup/500-mL) Prep Bowl**, whisk together soy sauce, ginger, oil, sugar and pressed garlic using **Stainless Mini Whisk**. Combine marinade and halibut in large resealable plastic bag; seal bag and turn carefully to coat. Refrigerate 20 minutes.

2 Meanwhile, thinly slice peas lengthwise using **Color Coated Chef's Knife**; set aside. Thinly slice green onions, separating white and light green bottoms from tops. Set aside onion tops for garnish, if desired. Thinly slice mushrooms and ginger; cut ginger slices into thin strips to measure 1 tbsp (15 mL).

3 Add oil to **(4-qt./3.8-L) Casserole**; heat over medium-high heat 1-3 minutes or until shimmering. Add onion bottoms, mushrooms, ginger and pressed garlic; cook 2-3 minutes or until mushrooms begin to soften. Add stock; cook, covered, 3-4 minutes or until gently boiling. Add noodles; cook, covered, 4-5 minutes or until noodles are tender, stirring occasionally. Stir in mirin, soy sauce and sugar. Remove Casserole from heat; stir in peas. Cover and set aside.

4 Heat **Grill Pan** over medium-high heat 3 minutes. Remove halibut from bag; discard marinade. Cook halibut 3 minutes on each side or until halibut flakes easily with a fork. Evenly divide broth and noodles among serving plates; top with halibut. Garnish with reserved green onion tops, if desired.

Cook's Tip

Mirin is a Japanese rice wine similar to sake but with a lower alcohol content. It is commonly used in Japanese cooking and adds sweetness to rice, sauces and dressings. It can be found in the Asian section of most grocery stores.

Ingredients

- 4   shallots, divided
- 4   4-in. (10-cm) sprigs fresh rosemary, divided
- 3   cups (750 mL) apple juice
- 1   cup (250 mL) cider vinegar
- 1   tsp (5 mL) whole black peppercorns
- ¼   cup (50 mL) pure maple syrup (do not use maple-flavored pancake syrup)
- ½   tsp (2 mL) salt, divided
- 2   tsp (10 mL) olive oil
- 1   tsp (5 mL) paprika
- ⅛   tsp (0.5 mL) coarsely ground black pepper
- 2   Cornish hens (1¼-1½ lbs/575-700 g each), giblets removed
- 2   sweet potatoes (about 14 oz/400 g), peeled

Nutrition Facts

Serving Size ½ hen (skin removed), ½ sweet potato, ½ T glaze
Servings Per Recipe 4

U.S. Nutrients Per Serving

Calories 420	Calories from Fat 60

	% Daily Value
Total Fat 7g	11%
Saturated Fat 1.5g	8%
Trans Fat 0g	
Cholesterol 120mg	40%
Sodium 420mg	18%
Total Carbohydrate 58g	19%
Dietary Fiber 3g	12%
Sugars 37g	
Protein 29g	

U.S. Diabetic Exchanges Per Serving

1½ starch, 2½ fruit, 3 low-fat meat (4 carb)

Apple-Glazed Cornish Hens

Cornish hens are infused with rosemary and shallots tucked under the skin. The apple-maple glaze gives the hens a rich, sweet flavor.

PREP TIME: 20 MINUTES   **TOTAL TIME:** 50 MINUTES   **YIELD:** 4 SERVINGS

1 For glaze, thinly slice two of the shallots using **Santoku Knife**. Place sliced shallots, two of the rosemary sprigs, juice, vinegar and peppercorns into **(10-in./24-cm) Skillet**. Boil over medium-high heat 20-25 minutes or until liquid reduces to ½ cup (125 mL). Strain glaze into **(2-cup/500-mL) Easy Read Measuring Cup** using **(5-in./13-cm) Strainer**. Discard solids. Return glaze to Skillet; add syrup and ¼ tsp (1 mL) of the salt. Reduce heat to medium; cook 2-3 minutes or until glaze is thickened, stirring frequently with **Silicone Flat Whisk**. Reserve 3 tbsp (45 mL) of the glaze for potatoes and garnish.

2 Preheat oven to 450°F (230°C). Line **Large Sheet Pan** with foil; set aside. Finely chop remaining shallots and rosemary leaves. Combine shallots, rosemary, remaining ¼ tsp (1 mL) salt, oil, paprika and black pepper in **(1-cup/250-mL) Prep Bowl**. Remove backbone from hen using **Professional Shears**. Cut in half along breastbone to make two halves. Trim wing tips and excess fat. Loosen skin from hen by inserting fingertips under skin and gently pushing between skin and meat. Season meat with shallot mixture. Repeat with remaining hen. Place hens skin-side up onto pan. Brush with half of the remaining glaze. Roast hens 20-25 minutes or until internal temperature reaches 165°F (74°C) in the thickest part of thigh and juices run clear, brushing with glaze after 10 minutes. (Discard any unused glaze.)

3 Meanwhile, slice sweet potatoes crosswise into ¼-in. (6-mm) pieces. Combine potatoes and ¼ cup (50 mL) water in **Large Micro-Cooker®**. Microwave, covered, on HIGH 4-6 minutes or until tender; drain. Add 1 tbsp (15 mL) of the reserved glaze to potatoes and toss gently. Serve hens with sweet potatoes and remaining 2 tbsp (30 mL) glaze.

Cook's Tips

The skin is left on the Cornish hens during cooking to add flavor to the seasoned meat but can be removed before serving for a heart-healthy main dish. The nutritional information reflects the hens with the skin removed.

Remove backbone from hens by cutting as close as possible down both sides of backbone using Professional Shears.

8	(6-in./15-cm) corn tortillas
⅛	tsp (0.5 mL) *each* salt and coarsely ground black pepper
3	medium navel oranges, segmented (see Cook's Tip)
1	medium avocado, diced
¼	small red onion, thinly sliced
¼	cup (50 mL) finely chopped fresh cilantro

SAUCE & STEAKS

4	cups (1 L) water
3	large dried ancho chile peppers, stemmed and seeded (see Cook's Tip)
¼	cup (50 mL) honey
2	tbsp (30 mL) red wine vinegar
1½	tbsp (22 mL) tomato paste
2	tsp (10 mL) Dijon mustard
1	garlic clove, peeled
¼	tsp (1 mL) *each* salt and coarsely ground black pepper, divided
4	boneless beef top sirloin steaks (3 oz/90 g each), cut ¾ in. (2 cm) thick

Nutrition Facts

Serving Size 1 steak, ¼ C sauce, ½ C salsa, 8 chips
Servings Per Recipe 4

U.S. Nutrients Per Serving

Calories 410	Calories from Fat 110
	% Daily Value
Total Fat 12g	**18%**
Saturated Fat 2.5g	**13%**
Trans Fat 0g	
Cholesterol 30mg	**10%**
Sodium 370mg	**15%**
Total Carbohydrate 57g	**19%**
Dietary Fiber 9g	**36%**
Sugars 22g	
Protein 22g	

U.S. Diabetic Exchanges Per Serving

1½ starch, 2½ fruit, 2½ low-fat meat (4 carb)

Sirloin Steaks with Ancho Chile Sauce & Citrus Salsa

Ancho chile peppers impart a mild heat to the sauce and steaks.

PREP TIME: 20 MINUTES   **TOTAL TIME:** 30 MINUTES   **YIELD:** 4 SERVINGS

1. For chips, preheat oven to 450°F (230°C). Using **Pizza Cutter**, cut each tortilla into four wedges. Lightly spray wedges with canola oil using **Kitchen Spritzer**; sprinkle with salt and black pepper. Place wedges on **Large Round Stone with Handles**, overlapping as necessary. Bake 12-15 minutes or until golden brown, turning every 5 minutes using **Slotted Turner**. Remove baking stone from oven to **Stackable Cooling Rack**. Meanwhile, for salsa, cut orange segments in half. Combine oranges, avocado, onion and cilantro in **Small Batter Bowl**; mix gently.

2. For sauce, place water and peppers into **(3-qt./2.8-L) Saucepan**. Bring to a boil; cook 3-4 minutes or until soft. Drain, reserving ¼ cup (50 mL) of the cooking liquid. Place peppers, cooking liquid, honey, vinegar, tomato paste, mustard, garlic and salt into blender container. Cover and blend until smooth. Reserve ¼ cup (50 mL) of the sauce in **(1-cup/250-mL) Prep Bowl** for steaks. Set remaining sauce aside until ready to serve.

3. Heat **Grill Pan** over medium-high heat 5 minutes. Brush tops of steaks with half of the reserved sauce using **Chef's Silicone Basting Brush**. Spray pan with canola oil using **Kitchen Spritzer**. Cook steaks, sauce side down, 3 minutes; brush steaks with remaining reserved sauce. (Discard any unused sauce.) Turn steaks over; cook 3 minutes or until internal temperature registers 140°F (60°C) for medium-rare doneness. Remove steaks from pan; sprinkle with black pepper. Tent steaks with foil and let stand 5 minutes (temperature will rise to 145°F (63°C). Spoon remaining sauce over steaks; serve with chips and salsa.

Cook's Tips

Dried ancho chile peppers, which are reddish peppers about 3-4 in. (7.5-10 cm) long, are actually dried poblano peppers. They are considered the sweetest of the dried chiles.

To remove stems and seeds from chile peppers before softening, cut peppers lengthwise using **Professional Shears** and pull open to remove seeds. Cut around tops of peppers to remove stems.

To cut orange into segments, cut a thin slice from the top and the bottom using **Utility Knife**; stand upright. Cutting from top to bottom, carefully trim away peel and white membrane. Cut down one side of membrane. Angle knife under segment and lift out. Repeat with remaining segments.

- 1 cup (250 mL) all-purpose flour, plus additional for dusting
- ½ cup (125 mL) whole wheat flour
- 1½ tbsp (22 mL) fresh rosemary leaves, finely chopped, divided
- 1 tsp (5 mL) active dry yeast
- ¼ tsp (1 mL) salt
- ½ cup (125 mL) warm water (110-120°F/43-49°C)
- 2 tsp (10 mL) olive oil, divided
- 1 tsp (5 mL) honey
- 6 oz (175 g) cooked Italian chicken sausage links (2 links)
- 2 plum tomatoes, seeded
- 2 garlic cloves, pressed
- 1 tbsp (15 mL) yellow cornmeal
- 1¾ oz (50 g) Provolone cheese
- ¼ tsp (1 mL) coarsely ground black pepper
- ¼ cup (50 mL) loosely packed fresh basil leaves, thinly sliced

Nutrition Facts

Serving Size ¼ pizza
Servings Per Recipe 4

U.S. Nutrients Per Serving

Calories 320	Calories from Fat 90
	% Daily Value
Total Fat 10g	15%
Saturated Fat 3.5g	18%
Trans Fat 0g	
Cholesterol 40mg	13%
Sodium 480mg	20%
Total Carbohydrate 40g	13%
Dietary Fiber 4g	16%
Sugars 2g	
Protein 17g	

U.S. Diabetic Exchanges Per Serving

2½ starch, ½ vegetable, 1 high-fat meat (2½ carb)

Chicken Sausage & Herb Wheat Pizza

With a quickly made crust, this pizza is faster and healthier than ordering out.

PREP TIME: 30 MINUTES   **TOTAL TIME:** 45 MINUTES   **YIELD:** 4 SERVINGS

1 Preheat oven to 450°F (230°C). Combine flours, 1 tbsp (15 mL) of the rosemary, yeast and salt in **Stainless (4-qt./4-L) Mixing Bowl**. Using **Stainless Mini Whisk**, whisk together water, 1 tsp (5 mL) of the oil and honey in **(2-cup/500-mL) Easy Read Measuring Cup**. Add water mixture to flour mixture; mix just until dough begins to come together using **Small Mix 'N Scraper®**. Turn dough out onto lightly-floured **Pastry Mat**. Knead dough 4-5 minutes or until smooth and elastic, but not sticky. Shape dough into a ball and return to mixing bowl; cover with plastic wrap. Let dough rise in warm place about 20 minutes.

2 Meanwhile, dice sausage and tomatoes, set aside. Combine remaining ½ tbsp (7 mL) rosemary, remaining 1 tsp (5 mL) oil and pressed garlic in **(1-cup/250-mL) Prep Bowl**. Sprinkle cornmeal over **Large Round Stone with Handles**. Place dough onto center of baking stone. Using **Baker's Roller®**, roll dough to within ½ in. (1 cm) of edge. Brush oil mixture over dough with **Chef's Silicone Basting Brush**. Bake 8-10 minutes or until crust is light golden brown.

3 Remove baking stone from oven to **Stackable Cooling Rack**. Top crust with sausage and tomatoes. Using **Rotary Grater**, grate cheese over pizza. Bake 4-6 minutes or until crust is deep golden brown and cheese is melted. Remove from oven; sprinkle with black pepper and basil.

Cook's Tip

To ensure a thin, crisp crust, do not let dough rise longer than 20 minutes.

- 2 medium shallots
- 1 tbsp (15 mL) capers, drained
- 1 lemon
- 2 tbsp (30 mL) light mayonnaise
- ½ tsp (2 mL) coarsely ground black pepper, divided
- 16 fresh asparagus spears (about 8 oz/250 g), trimmed
- 4 skinless salmon fillets (3 oz/90 g each)
- 1 tbsp (15 mL) **All-Purpose Dill Mix**
- 1 small fennel bulb (about 4 oz/125 g)
- 6 cups (1.5 L) mixed greens salad blend
- ¼ cup (50 mL) snipped fresh chives
- 1 can (14.5 oz or 398 mL) no-salt-added Great Northern beans, drained and rinsed

Nutrition Facts

Serving Size 1 fillet, ¼ C beans, 1½ C salad
Servings Per Recipe 4

U.S. Nutrients Per Serving

Calories 300	Calories from Fat 120
	% Daily Value
Total Fat 14g	22%
Saturated Fat 3g	15%
Trans Fat 0g	
Cholesterol 50mg	17%
Sodium 240mg	10%
Total Carbohydrate 22g	7%
Dietary Fiber 8g	32%
Sugars 4g	
Protein 23g	

U.S. Diabetic Exchanges Per Serving

1 starch, 1 vegetable, 2½ medium-fat meat (1 carb)

Fresh Herb Salad with Grilled Salmon

Calling up flavors of the Mediterranean, this salad is as beautiful as it is delicious.

PREP TIME: 10 MINUTES   **TOTAL TIME:** 25 MINUTES   **YIELD:** 4 SERVINGS

1 For dressing, finely chop shallots and capers with **Food Chopper**. Juice lemon with **Juicer** to measure 2 tbsp (30 mL). Combine shallots, capers, juice, mayonnaise and ¼ tsp (1 mL) of the black pepper in **(2-cup/500-mL) Prep Bowl**; mix well and set aside.

2 Heat **Grill Pan** over medium-high heat 5 minutes. Cook asparagus 2-3 minutes or until light grill marks appear. Remove asparagus from pan to **Cutting Board**; cool slightly. Cut asparagus into 1-in. (2.5-cm) pieces; set aside. Season salmon with dill mix. Cook salmon 2-2½ minutes on each side or until salmon flakes easily with a fork; remove from pan and let stand 5 minutes. Slice salmon into ½-in. (1-cm) pieces.

3 Trim fronds from fennel; snip fronds with **Professional Shears** and set aside. Slice fennel stalks and bulb crosswise into ⅛-inch-thick (3-mm) slices; cut slices in half. In **Stainless (6-qt./6-L) Mixing Bowl**, toss together asparagus, fennel, mixed greens, chives and dressing.

4 To serve, divide salad among serving plates. Top with beans and salmon; sprinkle with fennel fronds and remaining ¼ tsp (1 mL) black pepper.

Cook's Tip

If desired, 2 tbsp (30 mL) chopped fresh dill weed and ¼ tsp (1 mL) coarsely ground black pepper can be substituted for the All-Purpose Dill Mix.

6	garlic cloves, peeled
6	cups (1.5 L) unsalted chicken stock
1	oz (30 g) dried shiitake mushrooms, stems removed, broken into pieces
1	head baby bok choy, quartered lengthwise and cored
3	green onions with tops, divided
8	oz (250 g) 93% lean ground turkey
2	tbsp (30 mL) plus 2 tsp (10 mL) dry sherry, divided
1	tsp (5 mL) cornstarch
1	tsp (5 mL) grated fresh gingerroot
½	tsp (2 mL) ground white pepper
1	tsp (5 mL) toasted sesame oil (optional)
24	wonton wrappers
1	tbsp (15 mL) reduced-sodium soy sauce

Nutrition Facts

Serving Size 1¼ C soup, 4 wontons
Servings Per Recipe 6

U.S. Nutrients Per Serving

Calories 200	Calories from Fat 25
	% Daily Value
Total Fat 3g	5%
Saturated Fat 1g	5%
Trans Fat 0g	
Cholesterol 25mg	8%
Sodium 470mg	20%
Total Carbohydrate 26g	9%
Dietary Fiber 2g	8%
Sugars 1g	
Protein 17g	

U.S. Diabetic Exchanges Per Serving

1½ starch, 1 vegetable, 1 low-fat meat (1½ carb)

Turkey Wonton Soup

Aromatic ingredients like grated ginger, shiitake mushrooms and dry sherry mingle in this comforting Chinese-style soup.

PREP TIME: 25 MINUTES   **TOTAL TIME:** 50 MINUTES   **YIELD:** 6 SERVINGS

1 Slice garlic using **Garlic Slicer**. Combine garlic, stock and mushrooms in **(4-qt./3.8-L) Casserole**; bring to a simmer over medium heat. Remove from heat and set aside.

2 Slice bok choy crosswise using **Santoku Knife**; set aside. Thinly slice green onion tops; set aside. Finely chop green onion bottoms using **Food Chopper**. Combine onion bottoms, turkey, 2 tsp (10 mL) of the sherry, cornstarch, ginger, white pepper and oil, if using, in **Classic Batter Bowl**; mix well.

3 Spray **Stainless Steamer** with nonstick cooking spray. Arrange 12 wonton wrappers over flat side of **Large Grooved Cutting Board**. Spray with water using **Kitchen Spritzer**. Using **Small Scoop**, place a scant scoop of turkey mixture into center of each wonton. Gather corners to form a purse and place into Steamer. Repeat with remaining wonton wrappers and turkey mixture.

4 Bring 3 cups (750 mL) water to a boil in **(12-in./30-cm) Skillet**. Reduce heat to a simmer; place Steamer into Skillet. Cover; cook 5-7 minutes or until internal temperature of wontons reaches 165ºF (74ºC). Place four cooked wontons in each of six serving bowls.

5 Meanwhile, return stock to a simmer over medium heat. Stir in bok choy, onion tops, soy sauce and remaining 2 tbsp (30 mL) sherry. Ladle soup over wontons.

Cook's Tips

If desired, 2 cups (500 mL) chopped regular bok choy can be substituted for the baby bok choy.

Sherry is a fortified wine that is popular in Spain. For best results, choose a dry sherry that's suitable for drinking. Cooking sherry is not recommended for this recipe.

To fold wontons, gather the corners of the wonton wrapper around the turkey mixture, then pinch the top to form the purse.

ORZO & GREMOLATA

- 1 cup (250 mL) uncooked orzo pasta
- 1 orange
- 1 lemon, divided
- ¼ cup (50 mL) chopped fresh parsley
- 1 tsp (5 mL) olive oil
- 2 garlic cloves, pressed
- ⅛ tsp (0.5 mL) salt

CHICKEN & SAUCE

- 4 boneless, skinless chicken breasts (3 oz/90 g each)
- ½ tsp (2 mL) *each* salt and coarsely ground black pepper, divided
- 2 tsp (10 mL) olive oil, divided
- 2 tbsp (30 mL) all-purpose flour, divided
- 1 tsp (5 mL) paprika
- ¼ cup (50 mL) water
- 3 medium shallots, thinly sliced
- 3 garlic cloves, pressed
- ½ cup (125 mL) unsalted chicken stock
- ⅓ cup (75 mL) dry white wine such as Sauvignon Blanc
- 2 tbsp (30 mL) fresh lemon juice (from lemon used in gremolata)
- 2 tbsp (30 mL) unsalted butter

Lemon-Chicken Scallopine with Gremolata Orzo

Lemon plays a starring role in this pretty, guest-worthy entrée.

PREP TIME: 30 MINUTES   **TOTAL TIME:** 40 MINUTES   **YIELD:** 4 SERVINGS

1 Cook pasta according to package directions, omitting salt and oil; drain and place in **Small Batter Bowl**. Meanwhile, for gremolata, zest orange and lemon to measure 1 tsp (5 mL) zest *each*. Juice lemon to measure 2 tbsp (30 mL); set aside for later use in sauce. Combine zests, parsley, oil, pressed garlic and salt in **(2-cup/500-mL) Prep Bowl**; stir until combined. Add gremolata to orzo; toss to coat and set aside.

2 Meanwhile, for chicken, flatten chicken to an even thickness with **Meat Tenderizer**; season with ¼ tsp (1 mL) *each* of the salt and black pepper. Heat 1½ tsp (7 mL) of the oil in **Executive (12-in./30-cm) Skillet** (do not use stainless cookware) over medium-high heat 1-3 minutes or until shimmering. Combine 1½ tbsp (22 mL) of the flour and paprika in **Coating Tray**. Dredge chicken in flour mixture, coating evenly. Cook 3-4 minutes on each side or until centers are no longer pink. Remove chicken from Skillet; set aside and keep warm.

3 For sauce, whisk together remaining ½ tbsp (7 mL) flour and water until well blended in **(1-cup/250-mL) Easy Read Measuring Cup**. Add remaining ½ tsp (2 mL) oil, shallots and pressed garlic to Skillet. Cook 30-60 seconds or until fragrant, stirring occasionally. Add stock and wine; bring to a simmer. Add reserved 2 tbsp (30 mL) lemon juice and flour mixture, stirring constantly. Remove Skillet from heat; stir in butter and remaining ¼ tsp (1 mL) *each* salt and black pepper. Serve chicken with orzo; drizzle with sauce.

Cook's Tip

Gremolata is a garnish typically made with parsley, lemon zest and garlic.

Nutrition Facts

Serving Size 1 chicken breast, ⅔ C orzo, ¼ C sauce
Servings Per Recipe 4

U.S. Nutrients Per Serving

Calories 390	Calories from Fat 110

	% Daily Value
Total Fat 12g	18%
Saturated Fat 5g	25%
Trans Fat 0g	
Cholesterol 60mg	20%
Sodium 430mg	18%
Total Carbohydrate 42g	14%
Dietary Fiber 2g	8%
Sugars 3g	
Protein 25g	

U.S. Diabetic Exchanges Per Serving

3 starch, 2 medium-fat meat (3 carb)

- 6 small carrots, peeled
- 1½ cups (375 mL) grape tomatoes
- 1 small fennel bulb, stalks and fronds removed
- 1 medium shallot
- 1 lemon, divided
- ½ cup (125 mL) thinly sliced fresh basil leaves, divided
- 2 garlic cloves, pressed
- ½ tsp (2 mL) salt, divided
- ½ tsp (2 mL) coarsely ground black pepper, divided
- 4 skinless halibut fillets (4 oz/125 g each)
- 1 tbsp (15 mL) olive oil
- 1 tsp (5 mL) chopped fresh thyme leaves
- 4 tbsp (60 mL) dry white wine such as Sauvignon Blanc, divided

Nutrition Facts

Serving Size 1 pouch
Servings Per Recipe 4

U.S. Nutrients Per Serving

Calories 220	Calories from Fat 60
	% Daily Value
Total Fat 6g	9%
Saturated Fat 1g	5%
Trans Fat 0g	
Cholesterol 35mg	12%
Sodium 410mg	17%
Total Carbohydrate 13g	4%
Dietary Fiber 3g	12%
Sugars 5g	
Protein 26g	

U.S. Diabetic Exchanges Per Serving

2 vegetable, 3 low-fat meat (0 carb)

Tomato-Herb Halibut en Papillote

The delicate flavors of fennel and herbs permeate the fish and vegetables when using this healthy French style of cooking.

PREP TIME: 25 MINUTES   **TOTAL TIME:** 45 MINUTES   **YIELD:** 4 SERVINGS

1 Preheat oven to 425°F (220°C). Cut carrots into julienne strips using **Julienne Peeler**; set aside. Cut tomatoes into quarters using **Santoku Knife**. Thinly slice fennel bulb and finely chop shallot. Zest lemon using **Microplane® Zester** to measure 1 tsp (5 mL); set aside. Juice lemon using **Juicer** to measure 2 tbsp (30 mL).

2 Combine tomatoes, fennel, shallot, juice, ¼ cup (50 mL) of the basil, pressed garlic, ¼ tsp (1 mL) *each* of the salt and black pepper in **Classic Batter Bowl**; mix well. Brush fillets with oil using **Chef's Silicone Basting Brush**. Sprinkle with thyme, zest and remaining ¼ tsp (1 mL) *each* salt and black pepper.

3 To assemble, cut four 15-in. (38-cm) circles of **Parchment Paper** using **Professional Shears**. Arrange carrots evenly over center of each parchment circle. Top with tomato mixture, 1 tbsp (15 mL) of the wine and one fillet. Gather sides of parchment over fillet to create a pouch; tie with kitchen twine and place onto **Large Sheet Pan**.

4 Bake 14-18 minutes or until **Digital Pocket Thermometer** registers 135°F (57°C) when inserted through pouch into center of fillet. Remove pan from oven to **Stackable Cooling Rack**; let stand 5 minutes. (Temperature will rise to 145°F/60°C.) Place pouches onto serving plates; carefully cut open using Professional Shears. Garnish with remaining basil.

Cook's Tip

Fresh fennel is used widely in Italian and French dishes. The white bulb has a crisp, celery-like texture and a mild anise flavor.

1-2	limes, divided
½	cup (125 mL) plain nonfat yogurt, divided
2	tbsp (30 mL) chopped fresh cilantro, divided
¼	tsp (1 mL) plus ⅛ tsp (0.5 mL) salt, divided
½	small onion
1½	tsp (7 mL) ground coriander
1½	tsp (7 mL) ground cumin
1	tsp (5 mL) smoked paprika
2	garlic cloves, pressed
2	tsp (10 mL) grated fresh gingerroot
2	tsp (10 mL) tomato paste
2	tsp (10 mL) canola oil
8	turkey breast cutlets (about 1 lb/450 g)
¾	cup (175 mL) water
⅔	cup (150 mL) uncooked whole wheat couscous
1	medium zucchini (see Cook's Tip)

Nutrition Facts

Serving Size 2 cutlets, ½ C couscous,
2 T sauce, ¼ zucchini
Servings Per Recipe 4

U.S. Nutrients Per Serving

Calories 250	Calories from Fat 35
	% Daily Value
Total Fat 3.5g	5%
Saturated Fat 0g	0%
Trans Fat 0g	
Cholesterol 45mg	15%
Sodium 370mg	15%
Total Carbohydrate 23g	8%
Dietary Fiber 4g	16%
Sugars 4g	
Protein 33g	

U.S. Diabetic Exchanges Per Serving

1½ starch, 4 low-fat meat (1½ carb)

Skinny Turkey Tandoori

This well-spiced dish is made with turkey breast cutlets, which are one of the leanest cuts of meat.

PREP TIME: 20 MINUTES   **TOTAL TIME:** 50 MINUTES   **YIELD:** 4 SERVINGS

1 Zest limes using **Microplane® Adjustable Fine Grater** to measure 1 tsp (5 mL). Juice limes using **Citrus Press** to measure 2 tbsp (30 mL); set aside. For sauce, combine zest, ¼ cup (50 mL) of the yogurt, 1 tbsp (15 mL) of the cilantro and ⅛ tsp (0.5 mL) of the salt in **(1-cup/250-mL) Prep Bowl**. Mix well and set aside.

2 For marinade, finely chop onion using **Food Chopper**. Place coriander, cumin and paprika in **(8-in./20-cm) Sauté Pan**. Heat over medium-low heat 3-4 minutes or until fragrant, stirring constantly. In **Small Batter Bowl**, combine lime juice, remaining yogurt, onion, toasted spices, pressed garlic, ginger, tomato paste and oil; mix well. Place marinade and turkey in large resealable plastic bag; seal bag and turn carefully to coat. Refrigerate 30 minutes, up to 1 hour.

3 Place water in **Classic Batter Bowl**. Microwave on HIGH 60-90 seconds or until simmering; add couscous. Cover and let stand 5 minutes. Stir in remaining 1 tbsp (15 mL) cilantro; cover and keep warm.

4 Heat **Grill Pan** over medium-high heat 5 minutes. Remove turkey from bag; discard marinade. Season turkey with remaining ¼ tsp (1 mL) salt. Cut turkey to fit pan, if necessary. Add half of the turkey to pan. Top with **Grill Press** and cook 1-1½ minutes on each side or until grill marks appear. Remove from pan; repeat with remaining turkey. Serve with couscous, sauce and zucchini ribbons.

Cook's Tips

To make zucchini ribbons, cut ends from zucchini. Using **Vegetable Peeler**, slice down length of zucchini to make thin ribbons.

The marinade can be prepared a day in advance, if desired.

Toasting the spices intensifies their flavors and infuses them throughout the dish.

Zucchini Ribbon Primavera

- 2 tsp (10 mL) olive oil
- 3 large shallots
- 4 garlic cloves, pressed
- 3¼ cups (800 mL) unsalted chicken stock
- ¾ cup (175 mL) dry white wine such as Chardonnay
- ¼ tsp (1 mL) salt
- ¼ tsp (1 mL) coarsely ground black pepper
- 6 oz (175 g) uncooked protein-enriched multigrain thin spaghetti noodles
- 2 medium zucchini
- 2 medium carrots, peeled
- 1 medium red bell pepper
- ½ cup (125 mL) loosely packed fresh basil leaves
- 3 oz (90 g) reduced-fat cream cheese (Neufchâtel), softened
- ¾ oz (20 g) Parmesan cheese (see Cook's Tip)

Zucchini and carrots cut into fine julienne strips provide a colorful contrast to multigrain spaghetti for a fun pasta presentation.

PREP TIME: 10 MINUTES   **TOTAL TIME:** 20 MINUTES   **YIELD:** 4 SERVINGS

1. Heat oil in **Executive (12-in./30-cm) Skillet** (do not use stainless cookware) over medium-high heat 1-3 minutes or until shimmering. Finely chop shallots with **Food Chopper**. Add shallots and pressed garlic to Skillet; cook 30-45 seconds or until fragrant. Add stock, wine, salt and black pepper; cook, covered, 3-4 minutes or until simmering. Add noodles; cook, covered, 7-8 minutes or until noodles are tender, stirring occasionally.

2. Meanwhile, cut zucchini and carrots into julienne strips using **Julienne Peeler**. Thinly slice bell pepper and coarsely chop basil using **Chef's Knife**. Add cream cheese to Skillet; stir until fully incorporated using **Small Mix 'N Scraper®**. Remove Skillet from heat. Add zucchini, carrots, bell pepper and basil; toss gently with **Chef's Tongs**. Divide pasta among serving plates; garnish with shaved Parmesan cheese.

Cook's Tips

Substituting protein-enriched multigrain pasta for regular pasta in meatless recipes is an easy way to add protein and fiber into your diet.

Use **Vegetable Peeler** to shave Parmesan cheese.

Nutrition Facts

Serving Size 1¼ C pasta
Servings Per Recipe 4

U.S. Nutrients Per Serving

Calories 360	Calories from Fat 90

	% Daily Value
Total Fat 10g	15%
Saturated Fat 4g	20%
Trans Fat 0g	
Cholesterol 20mg	7%
Sodium 450mg	19%
Total Carbohydrate 42g	14%
Dietary Fiber 5g	20%
Sugars 5g	
Protein 18g	

U.S. Diabetic Exchanges Per Serving

2½ starch, 1 vegetable, 1 high-fat meat (2½ carb)

- 1 lb (450 g) red or yellow beets (about 4 small beets)
- 1 bunch fresh watercress (6 cups/1.5 L)
- 1 orange, divided
- 1-2 lemons, divided
- 2 tbsp (30 mL) light mayonnaise
- 4 skinless salmon fillets (3 oz/90 g each)
- ½ tsp (2 mL) salt, divided
- ½ tsp (2 mL) coarsely ground black pepper, divided
- 2 tsp (10 mL) honey
- 1 tbsp (15 mL) canola oil
- 2 tbsp (30 mL) chopped fresh chives

Nutrition Facts

Serving Size 1 fillet, 1½ C salad
Servings Per Recipe 4

U.S. Nutrients Per Serving

Calories 290	Calories from Fat 150
	% Daily Value
Total Fat 17g	26%
Saturated Fat 3g	15%
Trans Fat 0g	
Cholesterol 50mg	17%
Sodium 500mg	21%
Total Carbohydrate 16g	5%
Dietary Fiber 4g	16%
Sugars 11g	
Protein 20g	

U.S. Diabetic Exchanges Per Serving

2 vegetable, ½ fruit, 2½ medium-fat meat, ½ fat (½ carb)

Tangy Citrus Salmon with Beets & Watercress

Fresh, colorful and delicious, this salad is guaranteed to impress.

PREP TIME: 25 MINUTES   **TOTAL TIME:** 35 MINUTES   **YIELD:** 4 SERVINGS

1 Preheat broiler on HIGH. Line **Small Sheet Pan** with foil; set aside. Place beets and 2 cups (500 mL) water in **Large Micro-Cooker®**; microwave, covered, on HIGH 13-15 minutes or until tender. Fill **Stainless (6-qt./6-L) Mixing Bowl** halfway with ice water. Drain and immediately plunge beets into ice water. Let stand until chilled. Peel beets; cut into quarters. Slice beet quarters lengthwise into ½-in. (1-cm) pieces (see Cook's Tip). Place watercress into **Salad & Berry Spinner**. Rinse and spin dry. Set aside.

2 Meanwhile, zest orange and one lemon using **Microplane® Adjustable Fine Grater** to measure 2 tsp (10 mL) zest *each*. Juice orange to measure 2 tbsp (30 mL). Juice lemons to measure 1 tbsp (15 mL). Set juices aside. Combine mayonnaise and 1 tsp (5 mL) *each* of the orange and lemon zests in **(1-cup/250-mL) Prep Bowl**; mix well. Season salmon with ¼ tsp (1 mL) *each* of the salt and black pepper; place onto pan. Spread mayonnaise mixture over top of salmon. Broil 4-5 minutes or until salmon flakes easily with a fork.

3 For vinaigrette, combine reserved orange and lemon juices, remaining 1 tsp (5 mL) *each* orange and lemon zests, remaining ¼ tsp (1 mL) *each* salt and black pepper and honey in **Small Batter Bowl**. Slowly add oil, whisking until well blended. Combine beets, watercress and 3 tbsp (45 mL) of the vinaigrette in **Stainless (4-qt./4-L) Mixing Bowl**; toss gently using **Bamboo Salad Claws**. To serve, divide salad among serving plates; top with salmon. Drizzle with remaining vinaigrette; garnish with chives.

Cook's Tip

When handling fresh beets, be sure to wear plastic or latex gloves to prevent staining your hands.

8	oz (250 g) uncooked linguine pasta
1	pkg (14 oz or 397 g) extra-firm tofu, drained
3	tbsp (45 mL) reduced-sodium soy sauce, divided
1	can (13.5 oz/398 mL) light coconut milk
1½-2	tbsp (22-30 mL) Thai green curry paste
2	cups (500 mL) fresh asparagus spears
5	green onions with tops
1½	tsp (7 mL) toasted sesame oil, divided
2	cups (500 mL) fresh broccoli florets
1	tbsp (15 mL) grated fresh gingerroot
2	garlic cloves, pressed
½	cup (125 mL) frozen shelled edamame beans, thawed
½	cup (125 mL) chopped fresh cilantro

Nutrition Facts

Serving Size 2 C stir-fry
Servings Per Recipe 6

U.S. Nutrients Per Serving

Calories 310	Calories from Fat 90
	% Daily Value
Total Fat 10g	**15%**
Saturated Fat 3.5g	**18%**
Trans Fat 0g	
Cholesterol 0mg	**0%**
Sodium 440mg	**18%**
Total Carbohydrate 39g	**13%**
Dietary Fiber 5g	**20%**
Sugars 3g	
Protein 17g	

U.S. Diabetic Exchanges Per Serving

1 starch, 1 fruit, 2 vegetable,
1½ low-fat meat (2 carb)

Lean 'N Green Thai Stir-Fry

Marinated tofu, vegetables and a spicy green curry sauce make this meatless noodle dish a wake-up call for the senses.

PREP TIME: 15 MINUTES   **TOTAL TIME:** 25 MINUTES   **YIELD:** 6 SERVINGS

1 Cook pasta according to package directions, omitting salt and oil; drain. Meanwhile, pat tofu dry with paper towels, removing as much moisture as possible. Cut into ¾-in. (2-cm) cubes using **Santoku Knife**. Combine tofu and 1 tbsp (15 mL) of the soy sauce in **Classic Batter Bowl**; stir gently. Cover and set aside.

2 Combine coconut milk, curry paste and remaining 2 tbsp (30 mL) soy sauce in **Small Batter Bowl**; mix well and set aside. Cut asparagus diagonally into 1-in. (2.5-cm) pieces and green onions into ¾-in. (2-cm) pieces.

3 Heat ½ tsp (2 mL) of the oil in **(12-in./30-cm) Skillet** over medium heat 1-3 minutes or until shimmering. Add tofu to Skillet; cook 6-8 minutes or until browned on all sides, turning gently with **Slotted Turner**. Remove tofu from Skillet.

4 In same Skillet, heat remaining 1 tsp (5 mL) oil. Cook asparagus, green onions, broccoli, ginger and pressed garlic 3-4 minutes or until asparagus and broccoli are crisp-tender, stirring occasionally. Add pasta, tofu, coconut milk mixture and edamame to Skillet; cook 2-3 minutes or until heated through, tossing to coat. Remove Skillet from heat; add cilantro and mix well.

Cook's Tips

Heat levels of Thai green curry paste can vary. It's best to start with a lower amount and add more if desired.

To quickly thaw edamame for this recipe, place in large **Colander** and pour pasta over it to drain.

Patting the tofu dry helps to remove excess moisture and ensure even browning.

6	green onions with tops, divided
¼	cup (50 mL) reduced-sodium soy sauce
3	tbsp (45 mL) packed light brown sugar, divided
1	tbsp (15 mL) toasted sesame oil
1	tbsp (15 mL) grated fresh gingerroot, divided
4	garlic cloves, pressed, divided
1	lb (450 g) pork tenderloin
½	cup (125 mL) rice vinegar
1	tbsp (15 mL) Asian-style hot sauce such as Sriracha (optional)
¼	tsp (1 mL) salt
6	medium radishes
2	medium carrots, peeled
½	head Napa cabbage, thinly sliced (4 cups/1 L)
2	tbsp (30 mL) water
2	cups (500 mL) cooked jasmine rice (see Cook's Tip)

Nutrition Facts

Serving Size 3 medallions, ½ C rice, 1 C slaw
Servings Per Recipe 4

U.S. Nutrients Per Serving

Calories 270	Calories from Fat 30
	% Daily Value
Total Fat 3.5g	5%
Saturated Fat 1g	5%
Trans Fat 0g	
Cholesterol 75mg	25%
Sodium 350mg	15%
Total Carbohydrate 32g	11%
Dietary Fiber 3g	12%
Sugars 9g	
Protein 27g	

U.S. Diabetic Exchanges Per Serving

1 starch, 1 fruit, 3 low-fat meat (2 carb)

Korean Pork Tenderloin with Kimchi Slaw

This flavorful duo pairs savory pork with a spicy cabbage slaw that will leave a lasting impression.

PREP TIME: 20 MINUTES   **TOTAL TIME:** 45 MINUTES   **YIELD:** 4 SERVINGS

1   For marinade, thinly slice green onion tops; set aside. Finely chop onion bottoms using **Food Chopper**; place in **Classic Batter Bowl**. Add soy sauce, 1 tbsp (15 mL) of the brown sugar, oil, 2 tsp (10 mL) of the ginger and two of the pressed garlic cloves; mix well. Trim fat and silver skin from pork; cut pork crosswise into 1-in. (2.5-cm) medallions. Add pork to batter bowl and mix gently. Cover and refrigerate 30 minutes.

2   Meanwhile, for slaw, combine vinegar, hot sauce, if using, salt and remaining 2 tbsp (30 mL) sugar, 1 tsp (5 mL) ginger and pressed garlic in **Stainless (6-qt./6-L) Mixing Bowl**; mix well. On clean cutting board, slice radishes using **Ultimate Mandoline** fitted with adjustable blade on thick setting. Cut carrots into julienne strips using **Julienne Peeler**; cut into 1-in. (2.5-cm) pieces. Set aside 2 tbsp (30 mL) of the green onion tops for garnish. Add remaining onion tops, radishes, carrots and cabbage to mixing bowl; mix well.

3   Spray **(12-in./30-cm) Skillet** with canola oil using **Kitchen Spritzer**. Heat over medium heat 1-3 minutes or until shimmering. Remove pork from marinade; discard marinade. Add pork to Skillet; cook 2-3 minutes on each side or until golden brown. Add water; cover and cook 2-3 minutes or until water is evaporated. Serve pork with slaw and rice. Garnish with reserved green onion tops.

Cook's Tip

To prepare rice, combine 1 cup (250 mL) uncooked jasmine rice and 1¾ cups (425 mL) water in **Rice Cooker Plus**. Microwave on HIGH 10-12 minutes or until cooked. Let stand, covered, 10 minutes. Fluff with a fork and serve.

- 6 oz (175 g) uncooked multi-grain farfalle pasta (2 cups/500 mL)
- 1 lb (450 g) boneless, skinless chicken breasts
- ½ tsp (2 mL) plus ⅛ tsp (0.5 mL) salt, divided
- ½ tsp (2 mL) coarsely ground black pepper, divided
- 2 pints cherry tomatoes
- 1 tbsp (15 mL) olive oil
- 2 garlic cloves, pressed
- ½ cup (125 mL) chopped fresh basil leaves
- 1 tsp (5 mL) chopped fresh oregano leaves
- 3 cups (750 mL) fresh baby spinach leaves

Nutrition Facts

Serving Size 2 C pasta
Servings Per Recipe 4

U.S. Nutrients Per Serving

Calories 350	Calories from Fat 70
	% Daily Value
Total Fat 8g	12%
Saturated Fat 1.5g	8%
Trans Fat 0g	
Cholesterol 65mg	22%
Sodium 470mg	20%
Total Carbohydrate 37g	12%
Dietary Fiber 6g	24%
Sugars 4g	
Protein 33g	

U.S. Diabetic Exchanges Per Serving

2 starch, 1 vegetable, 3 low-fat meat (2 carb)

Chicken Farfalle Pomodoro

The fresh tomato sauce in this recipe is worth the extra effort and is healthier than most jarred varieties.

PREP TIME: 15 MINUTES   **TOTAL TIME:** 35 MINUTES   **YIELD:** 4 SERVINGS

1 Preheat broiler on HIGH. Cook pasta according to package directions, omitting salt and oil; drain and keep warm. Heat **Grill Pan** over medium heat 5 minutes. Lightly spray pan with olive oil using **Kitchen Spritzer**. Season chicken with ⅛ tsp (0.5 mL) of the salt and ¼ tsp (1 mL) of the black pepper. Place chicken into pan and top with **Grill Press**. Cook 5 minutes on each side or until internal temperature reaches 165°F (74°C) in thickest part of chicken and grill marks appear. Remove chicken from pan and dice with **Chef's Knife**.

2 Meanwhile, place tomatoes on **Medium Sheet Pan**; lightly spray with olive oil. Place pan 2-4 in. (5-10 cm) from heating element. Broil 2-3 minutes. Using **Oven Mitt**, carefully shake pan to turn tomatoes. Return pan to broiler; broil an additional 2-3 minutes or until tomatoes are slightly charred and just beginning to burst. Remove pan from oven to **Stackable Cooling Rack**.

3 In **Stainless (6-qt./6-L) Mixing Bowl**, combine tomatoes, oil, garlic pressed with **Garlic Press**, remaining ½ tsp (2 mL) salt and remaining ¼ tsp (1 mL) black pepper; mash gently with **Nylon Masher**. Add pasta, chicken, basil and oregano; toss to coat. Add spinach; toss gently. Serve immediately.

Cook's Tip

Farfalle pasta is also called bow tie pasta. If desired, other types of pasta, such as penne, can be substituted.

DESSERTS

VIENNESE-STYLE AMARETTO CHEESECAKE, PAGE 103

- 1 pkg (7 oz or 200 g) amaretti cookies (around 42 cookies), finely crushed (see Cook's Tip)
- 2 tbsp (30 mL) light butter, melted
- 1 pkg (16 oz) farmer's cheese (see Cook's Tip)
- 1 orange
- ¾ cup (175 mL) sugar, divided
- 3 tbsp (45 mL) all-purpose flour
- 4 large eggs, separated, divided
- ¼ cup (50 mL) 2% milk
- 2 tsp (10 mL) almond extract
- 1 lb (450 g) fresh strawberries, hulled
- 1 tbsp (15 mL) honey, warmed

Nutrition Facts

Serving Size 1 slice
Servings Per Recipe 16

U.S. Nutrients Per Serving

Calories 170	Calories from Fat 40
	% Daily Value
Total Fat 4.5g	7%
Saturated Fat 2g	10%
Trans Fat 0g	
Cholesterol 60mg	20%
Sodium 45mg	2%
Total Carbohydrate 27g	9%
Dietary Fiber 1g	4%
Sugars 12g	
Protein 6g	

U.S. Diabetic Exchanges Per Serving

1½ starch, ½ fruit, ½ fat (2 carb)

Viennese-Style Amaretto Cheesecake

Blending a homemade meringue with farmer's cheese gives this cheesecake the look of a traditional cheesecake but with less calories and fat.

PREP TIME: 20 MINUTES   **TOTAL TIME:** 8 HOURS OR OVERNIGHT   **YIELD:** 16 SLICES

1 Preheat oven to 325°F (160°C). For crust, lightly spray sides of **Springform Pan** with nonstick cooking spray. Line sides of pan with two 2½ x 13½-in. (6 x 34-cm) pieces of **Parchment Paper**. Combine cookie crumbs and butter in **Classic Batter Bowl**; stir until combined. Press crumb mixture onto bottom and slightly up sides of pan. Bake 12-14 minutes or until crust is slightly browned. Remove pan from oven to **Stackable Cooling Rack**.

2 For filling, place cheese in food processor; process until smooth. Using **Microplane® Adjustable Fine Grater**, zest orange to measure 1 tbsp (15 mL). In **Stainless (6-qt./6-L) Mixing Bowl**, combine zest, ½ cup (125 mL) of the sugar, flour, egg yolks, milk and extract. Beat on medium speed of electric hand mixer until smooth. Beat in cheese until smooth and creamy; set aside.

3 In **Stainless (4-qt./4-L) Mixing Bowl** and using clean beaters, beat egg whites on high speed until soft peaks form. While continuously beating, gradually add remaining ¼ cup (50 mL) sugar in a very slow, steady stream. Continue beating 3-4 minutes or until sugar is dissolved, meringue is glossy and stiff peaks form.

4 Stir one-fourth of the meringue into cheese mixture using **Small Mix 'N Scraper®**; gently fold in remaining meringue. Pour filling over crust. Bake 45-50 minutes or until center is set when gently shaken and top is very light golden brown. Remove pan from oven to cooling rack; cool 10 minutes. Remove collar and parchment from pan. Replace collar; cool completely, about 3 hours. Refrigerate 4 hours or overnight.

5 When ready to serve, slice strawberries using **Egg Slicer Plus®**. Top cheesecake with strawberries and brush with honey using **Chef's Silicone Basting Brush**.

Cook's Tips

Amaretti cookies are traditional Italian cookies that can be found in the cookie section of most grocery stores.

Farmer's cheese is a fresh white cheese that is often sold in a firm, solid loaf. It has a slightly tangy flavor. Look for cheese that has 1.5 g fat in 2 tbsp (30 mL).

For best results, top the cheesecake with strawberries just before serving.

CRUST

30	2½-in. (6-cm) chocolate wafer cookies
2	tbsp (30 mL) light butter, melted
1	tbsp (15 mL) water

MOUSSE

¼	cup (50 mL) plus 2 tbsp (30 mL) water, divided
2	tsp (10 mL) unflavored gelatin
½	cup (125 mL) fat-free half and half
½	cup (125 mL) sugar, divided
⅓	cup (75 mL) unsweetened cocoa powder
1	large egg, lightly beaten
1	tsp (5 mL) **Double-Strength Vanilla**
⅓	cup (75 mL) semi-sweet chocolate morsels
4	tsp (20 mL) dried egg whites (see Cook's Tip)
	Fresh strawberries (optional)

Nutrition Facts

Serving Size 1 slice
Servings Per Recipe 10

U.S. Nutrients Per Serving

Calories 200	Calories from Fat 60

	% Daily Value
Total Fat 7g	11%
Saturated Fat 3.5g	18%
Trans Fat 0g	
Cholesterol 25mg	8%
Sodium 190mg	8%
Total Carbohydrate 33g	11%
Dietary Fiber 2g	8%
Sugars 22g	
Protein 4g	

U.S. Diabetic Exchanges Per Serving

1¼ starch, 1 fruit, 1 fat (2¼ carb)

Decadent Chocolate Mousse Pie

This rich and creamy dessert is sure to satisfy any chocolate lover.

PREP TIME: 30 MINUTES   **TOTAL TIME:** 4 HOURS, 30 MINUTES OR OVERNIGHT
YIELD: 10 SERVINGS

1 Preheat oven to 350°F (180°C). Process cookies in two batches into fine crumbs using **Manual Food Processor**. Combine crumbs, butter and water in **Classic Batter Bowl**; mix just until moistened. Spread crumbs evenly over **(9-in./23-cm) Pie Plate**; using hands, firmly pack evenly onto bottom and up sides. Bake 9-11 minutes or until firm. Remove from oven to **Stackable Cooling Rack**; cool completely.

2 For mousse, place 2 tbsp (30 mL) of the water in **(1-cup/250-mL) Prep Bowl**. Sprinkle gelatin over water; stir until dissolved and set aside. Place half and half, ¼ cup (50 mL) of the sugar, cocoa powder, egg and vanilla in **(2-qt./1.9-L) Saucepan**. Cook over medium-low heat 6-8 minutes or until thickened and **Digital Pocket Thermometer** registers 160°F (71°C), stirring constantly with **Silicone Sauce Whisk**. Remove Saucepan from heat. Stir in gelatin mixture and chocolate morsels. Transfer chocolate mixture to **Stainless (4-qt./4-L) Mixing Bowl**. Refrigerate 10 minutes or until cooled to room temperature.

3 Combine remaining ¼ cup (50 mL) water and dried egg whites in **Stainless (2-qt./2-L) Mixing Bowl**. Whisk until egg whites are dissolved; beat on high speed of electric hand mixer until frothy. Add remaining ¼ cup (50 mL) sugar; beat until soft peaks form. Gently fold half of the meringue into chocolate mixture. Repeat with remaining meringue; fold until incorporated.

4 Pour mousse into pie shell. Refrigerate until mousse is set, 4 hours or overnight. Serve with strawberries, if desired.

Cook's Tips

Chocolate wafer cookies are thin and crisp. They can be found near the ice cream toppings in most grocery stores.

Dried egg whites are dried pasteurized egg whites. They are typically found in cans in the baking section of most grocery stores.

When cooking mousse, be sure to stir constantly to prevent the egg from curdling.

To accurately take the temperature of the mousse, briefly remove the Saucepan from heat, tilt it to move chocolate mixture to one side and insert Digital Pocket Thermometer so that 1 in. (2.5 cm) of the probe is submerged.

- 1 lemon, divided
- ¾ cup (175 mL) cake flour (do not use all-purpose flour)
- ½ cup (125 mL) sugar, divided
- ¾ tsp (4 mL) baking powder
- ¼ tsp (1 mL) salt
- 2 large egg yolks
- ¼ cup (50 mL) water
- 2½ tbsp (37 mL) canola oil
- 1 tbsp (15 mL) lemon extract
- 4 large egg whites, room temperature
  Meringue Frosting (see below)
- ½ cup (125 mL) prepared lemon curd

Nutrition Facts

Serving Size 1 cupcake
Servings Per Recipe 12

U.S. Nutrients Per Serving

Calories 190	Calories from Fat 40
	% Daily Value
Total Fat 4.5g	7%
Saturated Fat 1g	5%
Trans Fat 0g	
Cholesterol 45mg	15%
Sodium 125mg	5%
Total Carbohydrate 31g	10%
Dietary Fiber 0g	0%
Sugars 24g	
Protein 3g	

U.S. Diabetic Exchanges Per Serving

1 starch, 1 fruit, 1 fat (2 carb)

Lemon Chiffon Cupcakes

These cupcakes have a stylish flair that makes them suitable for special occasions, but we bet you'll enjoy them any time.

PREP TIME: 25 MINUTES   **TOTAL TIME:** 40 MINUTES   **YIELD:** 12 CUPCAKES

1 Preheat oven to 325°F (160°C). Place paper liners in wells of **Muffin Pan**. Using **Microplane® Adjustable Fine Grater**, zest lemon to measure 1½ tbsp (22 mL); set aside ½ tbsp (7 mL) zest for garnish. In **Stainless (2-qt./2-L) Mixing Bowl**, combine flour, ¼ cup (50 mL) of the sugar, baking powder, salt and remaining 1 tbsp (15 mL) zest; whisk well using **Stainless Whisk**. In **Stainless (6-qt./6-L) Mixing Bowl**, combine egg yolks, water, oil and extract; beat on medium speed of electric hand mixer until well blended. Add dry ingredients; beat on medium speed until smooth.

2 In **Stainless (4-qt./4-L) Mixing Bowl** and using clean beaters, beat egg whites on high speed until soft peaks form, about 1 minute. While continuously beating, gradually add remaining ¼ cup (50 mL) sugar in a very slow, steady stream. Continue beating 3-4 minutes or until sugar is dissolved and stiff peaks form. Stir in one-fourth of the meringue into batter using **Small Mix 'N Scraper®**; gently fold in remaining meringue.

3 Using **Large Scoop**, divide batter evenly among liners; bake 12-15 minutes or until wooden pick inserted in centers comes out clean. Remove pan from oven to **Stackable Cooling Rack**. Remove cupcakes from pan; cool completely. Meanwhile, prepare *Meringue Frosting* (see below).

4 To assemble cupcakes, spoon lemon curd into **Easy Accent® Decorator** fitted with closed star tip. Press decorator gently into center of each cupcake and pipe in a small amount of curd (about 2 tsp/10 mL). Frost cupcakes; sprinkle with reserved lemon zest.

MERINGUE FROSTING

- 3 large egg whites
- ¼ tsp (1 mL) cream of tartar
- ½ cup (125 mL) sugar
- 1 tsp (5 mL) lemon extract

Bring 2½ cups (625 mL) water to a simmer over medium-low heat in **(3-qt./2.8-L) Saucepan**. Place egg whites in **Double Boiler**; set over water in Saucepan. Using electric hand mixer, beat egg whites on high speed until frothy; beat in cream of tartar. While continuously beating, gradually add sugar in a very slow, steady stream. Continue beating until mixture is thickened and **Digital Pocket Thermometer** registers 160°F (71°C); carefully remove boiler from Saucepan. Continue beating until mixture is glossy and stiff peaks form; beat in lemon extract. Spoon frosting into resealable plastic bag. Twist bag to seal. Cut off corner and pipe over cupcakes.

- ¾ cup (175 mL) dried apricots
- ¼ cup (50 mL) plus 1 tsp (5 mL) canola oil, divided
- 2 tbsp (30 mL) packed brown sugar
- 1¼ cups (300 mL) all-purpose flour
- ¾ cup (175 mL) granulated sugar
- ¼ cup (50 mL) yellow cornmeal
- 1 tsp (5 mL) baking powder
- ½ tsp (2 mL) baking soda
- ½ tsp (2 mL) salt
- 2 large eggs
- ½ cup (125 mL) low-fat buttermilk
- ⅓ cup (75 mL) unsweetened applesauce
- 1 tsp (5 mL) **Double-Strength Vanilla**
- 1 tbsp (15 mL) orange zest (optional)

Nutrition Facts

Serving Size 1 slice
Servings Per Recipe 10

U.S. Nutrients Per Serving

Calories 260	Calories from Fat 70
	% Daily Value
Total Fat 7g	11%
Saturated Fat 1g	5%
Trans Fat 0g	
Cholesterol 45mg	15%
Sodium 260mg	11%
Total Carbohydrate 45g	15%
Dietary Fiber 2g	8%
Sugars 27g	
Protein 4g	

U.S. Diabetic Exchanges Per Serving

1 starch, 2 fruit, 1 fat (3 carb)

Warm Apricot Cake

Sweeten up your afternoon with a warm slice of this rustic cake.

PREP TIME: 20 MINUTES   **TOTAL TIME:** 1 HOUR, 10 MINUTES   **YIELD:** 10 SLICES

1 Preheat oven to 350°F (180°C). Combine apricots and 2 cups (500 mL) water in **Large Micro-Cooker®**. Microwave, covered, on HIGH 10 minutes or until apricots are softened. Let stand, covered, 10 minutes; drain. Brush sides and bottom of **Executive (10-in./24-cm) Skillet** (do not use stainless cookware) with 1 tsp (5 mL) of the oil. Sprinkle brown sugar over bottom of Skillet. Arrange apricots over sugar.

2 Meanwhile, combine flour, granulated sugar, cornmeal, baking powder, baking soda and salt in **Classic Batter Bowl**. Using electric hand mixer on medium speed, beat remaining ¼ cup (50 mL) oil, eggs, buttermilk, applesauce, vanilla and zest, if using, until well blended in **Stainless (4-qt./4-L) Mixing Bowl**. Gradually add dry ingredients; beat an additional 60-90 seconds or until smooth. Carefully pour batter over apricots, spreading evenly.

3 Bake 30-35 minutes or until wooden pick inserted in center comes out clean. Using **Oven Mitts**, carefully remove Skillet from oven; let stand 10 minutes. Carefully invert cake onto **Cake Pedestal** and cool 10 minutes; serve warm.

Cook's Tip

If desired, 2 tsp (10 mL) regular vanilla extract can be substituted for the Double-Strength Vanilla.

SAUCE

- ⅓ cup (75 mL) 2% milk
- ¼ cup (50 mL) unsweetened cocoa powder
- ¼ cup (50 mL) sugar
- 1 tsp (5 mL) **Double-Strength Vanilla**

PANNA COTTA

- 1 cup (250 mL) 2% milk
- 1½ tbsp (22 mL) unflavored gelatin
- 3 tbsp (45 mL) instant espresso powder
- 1¾ cups (425 mL) low-fat half and half
- 1 can (14 oz/300 mL) sweetened condensed milk
- ½ tsp (2 mL) **Double-Strength Vanilla**

  Unsweetened cocoa powder for dusting

  Chocolate-covered espresso beans and additional unsweetened cocoa powder (optional)

Nutrition Facts

Serving Size 1 slice
Servings Per Recipe 12

U.S. Nutrients Per Serving

Calories 180	Calories from Fat 45
	% Daily Value
Total Fat 5g	8%
Saturated Fat 3.5g	18%
Trans Fat 0g	
Cholesterol 15mg	5%
Sodium 70mg	3%
Total Carbohydrate 27g	9%
Dietary Fiber 1g	4%
Sugars 25g	
Protein 6g	

U.S. Diabetic Exchanges Per Serving

1 starch, 1 fruit, 1 fat (2 carb)

Espresso Panna Cotta

The smooth texture and the rich flavor of this no-bake dessert are sure to delight your guests.

PREP TIME: 10 MINUTES   **TOTAL TIME:** 6 HOURS, 25 MINUTES OR OVERNIGHT
YIELD: 12 SERVINGS

1 For sauce, whisk together milk, cocoa powder and sugar in **(1.5-qt./1.4-L) Saucepan**. Bring mixture to a boil over medium-high heat, stirring constantly. Reduce heat to medium-low and boil gently 4-5 minutes or until slightly thickened, stirring constantly. Remove from heat; stir in vanilla. Carefully pour sauce into **(1-cup/250-mL) Prep Bowl**. Cool to room temperature; cover and refrigerate until ready to serve.

2 For panna cotta, lightly spray inside of **Cake Pan** with nonstick cooking spray. Place milk in **(2-qt./1.9-L) Saucepan**. Sprinkle gelatin over milk and let stand 5 minutes to soften. Cook over medium heat until gelatin is dissolved, stirring constantly. Add espresso powder; stir until dissolved. Remove from heat and stir in half and half, condensed milk and vanilla. Pour mixture into pan. Refrigerate, uncovered, until cold. Cover and refrigerate until set, at least 6 hours or overnight.

3 To unmold, run a small plastic knife around edge of pan. Dip bottom of pan into warm water about 30 seconds to help loosen. To prevent panna cotta from forming another seal, place a small piece of **Parchment Paper** between panna cotta and edge of pan. Sprinkle panna cotta with cocoa powder using **Flour/Sugar Shaker**. Place **Cake Pedestal** upside-down over top of pan; carefully invert onto center of platter. Remove pan and parchment; lightly sprinkle edge of platter with cocoa powder.

4 To serve, cut panna cotta into wedges using **Utility Knife** dipped in warm water and dried slightly. Place wedge on serving plate; drizzle with scant 1 tbsp (15 mL) sauce. If desired, garnish with espresso bean and sprinkle with additional cocoa powder.

Cook's Tips

This panna cotta should be inverted on a flat serving platter or plate that will allow it to lie flat and make it easier to slice and serve.

For easiest release from pan, be sure to place a small piece of Parchment Paper between side of the pan and panna cotta. This prevents the panna cotta from sealing itself back to the edge of the pan.

Sprinkle panna cotta liberally with additional cocoa powder before unmolding onto serving platter or plate, making it easier for serving.

CRÊPES

- 1 cup (250 mL) all-purpose flour
- 1 cup (250 mL) 1% milk
- ½ cup (125 mL) water
- ½ cup (125 mL) pasteurized refrigerated egg product
- 1 tbsp (15 mL) sugar
- 2 tsp (10 mL) light butter, melted
- 1 tsp (5 mL) **Double-Strength Vanilla**

FILLING & SAUCE

- 2 tsp (10 mL) light butter
- 1¼ tsp (6 mL) grated fresh gingerroot
- 1½ lbs (700 g) fresh nectarines, pitted and sliced (5-6 nectarines)
- 4½ tbsp (67 mL) packed brown sugar, divided
- 1 tbsp (15 mL) fresh lemon juice
- 1 tsp (5 mL) **Cinnamon Plus®** **Spice Blend**
- ½ cup (125 mL) reduced-fat sour cream
- 1 tsp (5 mL) Double-Strength Vanilla
- 2 tbsp (30 mL) toasted sliced almonds (optional)

Nutrition Facts

Serving Size 2 filled crêpes
Servings Per Recipe 6

U.S. Nutrients Per Serving

Calories 250	Calories from Fat 40
	% Daily Value
Total Fat 5g	8%
Saturated Fat 2.5g	13%
Trans Fat 0g	
Cholesterol 15mg	5%
Sodium 95mg	4%
Total Carbohydrate 45g	15%
Dietary Fiber 2g	8%
Sugars 25g	
Protein 7g	

U.S. Diabetic Exchanges Per Serving

1 starch, 2 fruit, ½ low-fat meat, ½ fat (3 carb)

Sweet Crêpes with Ginger-Nectarine Filling

Fresh nectarines make a tantalizing filling for these dessert crêpes.

PREP TIME: 20 MINUTES   **TOTAL TIME:** 50 MINUTES   **YIELD:** 6 SERVINGS

1 Combine crêpe ingredients in **Classic Batter Bowl**; whisk until smooth. Cover and refrigerate 30 minutes (see Cook's Tip).

2 Meanwhile, for filling, melt butter in **Executive (10-in./24-cm) Skillet** (do not use stainless cookware) over medium heat. Add ginger to Skillet; cook 30-45 seconds or until fragrant. Add nectarines, 2½ tbsp (37 mL) of the brown sugar, lemon juice and spice blend to Skillet; cook, uncovered, 3-4 minutes or until nectarines are softened, stirring occasionally. Remove Skillet from heat.

3 Using **Kitchen Spritzer**, lightly spray **Executive (8-in./20-cm) Sauté Pan** (do not use stainless cookware) with canola oil. Heat pan over medium heat 1-3 minutes or until shimmering. Pour scant ¼ cup (50 mL) crêpe batter into pan, immediately tilting and swirling pan to cover bottom. When crêpe starts to bubble and edges are brown, turn using **Small Slotted Turner**. Cook additional 1 minute or until lightly browned. Remove from pan. Repeat with remaining batter, lightly spraying pan with additional oil every other crêpe.

4 For sauce, combine sour cream, vanilla and remaining 2 tbsp (30 mL) brown sugar in **(2-cup/500-mL) Prep Bowl**; stir until sugar is dissolved. To assemble, drizzle 1 tsp (5 mL) sauce over one crêpe; top with scant ¼ cup (50 mL) filling. Fold crêpe to form a square. Top with 1 tbsp (15 mL) filling and 1 tsp (5 mL) sauce; repeat with remaining crêpes, filling and sauce. Sprinkle with almonds, if desired.

Cook's Tips

Pumpkin pie spice can be substituted for the Cinnamon Plus® Spice Blend, if desired.

Allowing the crêpe batter to rest gives the flour time to absorb into the liquid, eliminating air bubbles, which results in stronger, more elastic crêpes.

- ⅓ cup (75 mL) plus 2 tbsp (30 mL) sugar, divided
- 2 large eggs, divided
- 1-2 oranges, divided
- ¼ cup (50 mL) honey
- ⅓ cup (75 mL) low-fat buttermilk
- 2 tbsp (30 mL) orange liqueur
- ½ cup (125 mL) all-purpose flour
- ⅛ tsp (0.5 mL) salt
- ¼ tsp (1 mL) cream of tartar
- 1 cup (250 mL) fresh blackberries

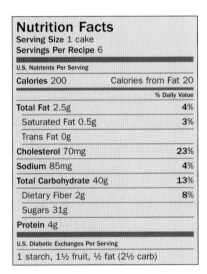

Nutrition Facts

Serving Size 1 cake
Servings Per Recipe 6

U.S. Nutrients Per Serving

Calories 200	Calories from Fat 20
	% Daily Value
Total Fat 2.5g	4%
Saturated Fat 0.5g	3%
Trans Fat 0g	
Cholesterol 70mg	23%
Sodium 85mg	4%
Total Carbohydrate 40g	13%
Dietary Fiber 2g	8%
Sugars 31g	
Protein 4g	

U.S. Diabetic Exchanges Per Serving

1 starch, 1½ fruit, ½ fat (2½ carb)

Mini Honey-Glazed Orange Pudding Cakes

A few ingredients are all that's needed to create these moist and tender cakes.

PREP TIME: 10 MINUTES   **TOTAL TIME:** 40 MINUTES   **YIELD:** 6 SERVINGS

1 Preheat oven to 350°F (180°C). Spray six **(1-cup/250-mL) Prep Bowls** with canola oil using **Kitchen Spritzer**. Coat evenly with 2 tbsp (30 mL) of the sugar. Arrange Prep Bowls in **Rectangle Baking Pan**; set aside. Separate eggs using **Egg Separator**, placing whites into **Stainless (2-qt./2-L) Mixing Bowl** and yolks into **Classic Batter Bowl**. Set whites aside.

2 Zest oranges using **Microplane® Adjustable Fine Grater** to measure 1 tbsp (15 mL) plus ½ tsp (2 mL). For glaze, combine ½ tsp (2 mL) of the zest and honey in **(1-cup/250-mL) Easy Read Measuring Cup**; set aside. Add remaining 1 tbsp (15 mL) zest, buttermilk and orange liqueur to yolks in batter bowl; whisk until combined. Add flour and salt; whisk until smooth.

3 Add cream of tartar to egg whites in mixing bowl; beat on high speed of electric hand mixer 30 seconds. Add remaining ⅓ cup (75 mL) sugar; beat 3-5 minutes or until soft peaks form and mixture is glossy. Fold one-third of the egg white mixture into yolk mixture using **Stainless Whisk**; repeat with remaining egg white mixture.

4 Divide batter evenly among Prep Bowls using **Large Scoop**. Carefully pour 2 cups (500 mL) hot water into pan. Bake 25-28 minutes or until wooden pick inserted in centers comes out clean. Carefully remove bowls from pan using **Chef's Tongs** and immediately invert onto serving plates; remove bowls. Microwave glaze on HIGH 10-15 seconds or until warm. Serve cakes with glaze and blackberries.

Cook's Tip

Use a gentle folding motion when incorporating the egg white mixture into yolk mixture. This will provide a soufflé-like texture to these tender cakes.

4 oz (125 g) fine-quality semi-sweet chocolate, finely chopped

2½ tbsp (37 mL) seedless raspberry jam, divided

1 tsp (5 mL) almond extract

12 sheets (9 x 14 in./23 x 35 cm) thawed frozen phyllo dough

2 tsp (10 mL) sugar, divided

1 cup (250 mL) fresh raspberries

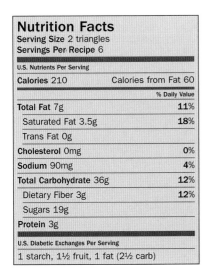

Nutrition Facts

Serving Size 2 triangles
Servings Per Recipe 6

U.S. Nutrients Per Serving

Calories 210	Calories from Fat 60
	% Daily Value
Total Fat 7g	11%
Saturated Fat 3.5g	18%
Trans Fat 0g	
Cholesterol 0mg	0%
Sodium 90mg	4%
Total Carbohydrate 36g	12%
Dietary Fiber 3g	12%
Sugars 19g	
Protein 3g	

U.S. Diabetic Exchanges Per Serving

1 starch, 1½ fruit, 1 fat (2½ carb)

Raspberry-Chocolate Truffle Triangles

Crispy phyllo pastry packets bursting with a raspberry-infused, creamy filling spells pure indulgence.

PREP TIME: 15 MINUTES   **TOTAL TIME:** 1 HOUR   **YIELD:** 6 SERVINGS

1 Preheat oven to 375°F (190°C). Place chocolate and 2 tbsp (30 mL) of the jam in **Small Batter Bowl**. Microwave, uncovered, on HIGH 30-45 seconds or until chocolate is mostly melted. Add almond extract; stir until smooth with **Small Mix 'N Scraper®**. Refrigerate, uncovered, 30 minutes, stirring occasionally.

2 Stack two phyllo sheets on top of each other on flat side of **Large Grooved Cutting Board**. Spray with nonstick cooking spray; place two additional sheets over first, pressing sheets together to seal. Sprinkle with ½ tsp (2 mL) of the sugar. Cut stack crosswise into four strips using **Pizza Cutter**.

3 Using **Small Scoop**, place a scant scoop of chocolate filling on one end of each strip. Fold corner of strip up to form a triangle. Continue folding back and forth (as you would fold a flag) until you reach the end of the strip, forming a filled triangle packet. Repeat with remaining phyllo sheets, cooking spray, sugar and chocolate filling for a total of 12 triangles. (Reserve remaining chocolate filling for use as sauce.) Sprinkle triangles with remaining ½ tsp (2 mL) sugar.

4 Place triangles on **Cookie Sheet**; bake 12-14 minutes or until golden brown. Remove from oven; cool 5 minutes. Add remaining ½ tbsp (7 mL) jam to reserved chocolate filling in batter bowl. Microwave on HIGH 10 seconds; stir until smooth. Drizzle sauce over triangles. Garnish with raspberries.

Cook's Tip

Phyllo dough comes in various sizes. Be sure to purchase phyllo that is 9 x 14 in. (23 x 35 cm) for this recipe.

1 lb (450 g) fresh strawberries, quartered

2 medium fresh peaches, peeled, pitted and diced

1 cup (250 mL) water

½ cup (125 mL) pulp-free orange juice

⅓ cup (75 mL) sugar

1 large sprig fresh basil

1 tbsp (15 mL) fresh lemon juice

1 tsp (5 mL) lemon zest

1 tsp (5 mL) grated fresh gingerroot

½ cup (125 mL) chilled dry champagne

RASPBERRY SAUCE & FRUIT GARNISH

1 pint fresh raspberries (about 2 cups/500 mL)

3 tbsp (45 mL) sugar

1½ tsp (7 mL) fresh lemon juice

8 oz (250 g) fresh strawberries, halved

1 medium fresh peach, pitted and thinly sliced

Nutrition Facts

Serving Size 1 ice mold, about 1 T sauce
Servings Per Recipe 12

U.S. Nutrients Per Serving

Calories 90	Calories from Fat 5

	% Daily Value
Total Fat 0g	0%
Saturated Fat 0g	0%
Trans Fat 0g	
Cholesterol 0mg	0%
Sodium 0mg	0%
Total Carbohydrate 21g	7%
Dietary Fiber 3g	12%
Sugars 16g	
Protein 1g	

U.S. Diabetic Exchanges Per Serving

1½ fruit (1½ carb)

Summer Fruit Ice Molds with Fresh Raspberry Sauce

This eye-catching dessert is sure to cool you off on a hot summer day!

PREP TIME: 30 MINUTES **TOTAL TIME:** 2 HOURS, 30 MINUTES **YIELD:** 12 SERVINGS

1 For ice molds, combine strawberries, peaches, water, orange juice, sugar, basil, lemon juice, lemon zest and ginger in **(4-qt./3.8-L) Casserole**. Cook, uncovered, over medium-high heat until fruit mixture comes to a boil. Reduce heat to low; cook, covered, 15 minutes. Carefully pour hot fruit mixture into **Stainless (4-qt./4-L) Mixing Bowl**; cool 10 minutes. Remove and discard basil.

2 Pour fruit mixture into blender container. Cover and blend until smooth; carefully stir in champagne. Pour into wells of **Silicone Floral Cupcake Pan**; freeze 2 hours or until firm.

3 Meanwhile, for sauce, combine raspberries, sugar and lemon juice in **(1.5-qt./1.4-L) Saucepan**. Cook, uncovered, over medium heat 7-9 minutes or until sauce is thickened, stirring occasionally. Carefully strain sauce using **(7-in./18-cm) Strainer** into **Small Batter Bowl**, pressing down to release juices, discard seeds. Cover and refrigerate until ready to serve.

4 To serve, drizzle sauce over serving plates; top with ice mold and garnish with strawberry halves and peach slices.

Cook's Tips

If desired, 1 lb (450 g) frozen unsweetened strawberries and 10 oz (300 g) frozen unsweetened sliced peaches (about 20 slices) can be substituted for the fresh strawberries and peaches in the ice molds.

Frozen unsweetened raspberries can be substituted for the fresh raspberries in the raspberry sauce, if desired.

Ice molds can be prepared up to 24 hours in advance. Remove cupcake pan from freezer 30 minutes before serving to allow ice molds to soften to desired consistency.

- ⅓ cup (75 mL) sugar
- ¼ cup (50 mL) water
- 1 bag (12 oz) sweetened frozen mixed berries (2¾ cups/675 mL)
- 1 cup (250 mL) plain 3.5% fat Greek yogurt
- 2 tbsp (30 mL) honey
- ⅛ tsp (0.5 mL) **Double-Strength Vanilla**
- 1 cup (250 mL) fresh blueberries
- Fresh mint leaves (optional)

Nutrition Facts

Serving Size 1 parfait
Servings Per Recipe 4

U.S. Nutrients Per Serving

Calories 240	Calories from Fat 50
	% Daily Value
Total Fat 6g	9%
Saturated Fat 4.5g	23%
Trans Fat 0g	
Cholesterol 10mg	3%
Sodium 20mg	1%
Total Carbohydrate 44g	15%
Dietary Fiber 4g	16%
Sugars 37g	
Protein 5g	

U.S. Diabetic Exchanges Per Serving

2 fruit, 1 medium-fat milk (3 carb)

Berry Granita Parfaits

Honey-kissed yogurt is layered with frosty granita for a luscious, cool parfait.

PREP TIME: 20 MINUTES   **TOTAL TIME:** 2 HOURS, 15 MINUTES   **YIELD:** 4 SERVINGS

1 For syrup, combine sugar and water in **(2-cup/500-mL) Prep Bowl**. Microwave on HIGH 2-3 minutes or until steaming and sugar is dissolved; set aside.

2 Place berries into **Classic Batter Bowl**; microwave 30-45 seconds or until berries are slightly thawed. Place half of the berries into **Manual Food Processor**; cover and pump handle until coarsely chopped, scraping down sides as necessary. Add remaining berries and syrup in processor; pump handle until smooth. Press berry mixture through **(7-in./18-cm) Strainer** into **Stainless (4-qt./4-L) Mixing Bowl** using **Classic Scraper**; discard seeds.

3 Place berry mixture in freezer; freeze 2-3 hours, stirring every 30 minutes with **Mix 'N Chop** until completely frozen and mixture appears finely chopped.

4 Combine yogurt, honey and vanilla in another (2-cup/500-mL) Prep Bowl. For each serving, place 2 tbsp (30 mL) of the granita in each of four **Dots Martini Glasses**. Layer with ¼ cup (50 mL) of the yogurt mixture, 2 tbsp (30 mL) of the blueberries, ¼ cup (50 mL) of the granita and 2 tbsp (30 mL) of the blueberries. Garnish with mint leaves, if desired.

Cook's Tip

Both the granita and the yogurt mixture can be prepared a day in advance. Cover and store granita in the freezer and yogurt mixture in the refrigerator.

1 cup (250 mL) all-purpose flour

2 tsp (10 mL) sugar

⅛ tsp (0.5 mL) salt

1 cup (250 mL) water

1½ tbsp (22 mL) unsalted butter

3 large egg whites

1 large egg yolk

FILLING AND GARNISH

1½ cups (375 mL) light vanilla ice cream, softened (see Cook's Tip)

3 tbsp (45 mL) sliced almonds, toasted

½ cup (125 mL) **Caramel Sauce**, divided

½ tsp (2 mL) **Coarse Sea & Himalayan Salt**

Nutrition Facts

Serving Size 2 filled cream puffs
Servings Per Recipe 6

U.S. Nutrients Per Serving

Calories 270	Calories from Fat 80
	% Daily Value
Total Fat 8g	12%
Saturated Fat 4.5g	23%
Trans Fat 0g	
Cholesterol 55mg	18%
Sodium 310mg	13%
Total Carbohydrate 43g	14%
Dietary Fiber 1g	4%
Sugars 2g	
Protein 7g	

U.S. Diabetic Exchanges Per Serving

2 starch, 1 fruit, 1 fat (3 carb)

Cream Puffs with Caramel Swirl Ice Cream

A light sprinkling of salt enhances the creamy sweetness of the ice cream in this sweet and salty indulgence.

PREP TIME: 25 MINUTES   **TOTAL TIME:** 1 HOUR, 10 MINUTES   **YIELD:** 6 SERVINGS

1 Preheat oven to 400°F (200°C). Line **Cookie Sheet** with **Parchment Paper**; set aside. Combine flour, sugar and salt in **Stainless (4-qt./4-L) Mixing Bowl**. Bring water and butter to a boil in **(3-qt./2.8-L) Saucepan** over medium-high heat; add dry ingredients. Reduce heat to medium-low. Stir vigorously about 1 minute or until mixture leaves sides of Saucepan and forms into a ball. Place dough in mixing bowl; cool 5 minutes. Using electric hand mixer on low speed, beat in egg whites and yolk, one at a time, beating after each addition until smooth (see Cook's Tip).

2 Using **Medium Scoop**, drop 12 level scoops of dough onto Cookie Sheet. Bake 35-40 minutes or until deep golden brown; remove Cookie Sheet from oven to **Stackable Cooling Rack**. Carefully pierce the side of each puff with **Paring Knife**. Turn oven off. Return puffs to oven 5 minutes, leaving oven door partially open. Remove puffs from oven to cooling rack; cool completely.

3 Meanwhile, combine ice cream and almonds in **Small Batter Bowl**; stir in ¼ cup (50 mL) of the caramel sauce. Freeze 25-30 minutes or until firm.

4 Using **Color Coated Bread Knife**; slice puffs in half horizontally. Using **Ice Cream Dipper**, scoop ice cream onto puff bottoms; top with puff tops. Drizzle with remaining caramel sauce; sprinkle with salt. Let stand 3-4 minutes before serving.

Cook's Tips

Look for light ice cream that has 100 calories (or less), 3 g total fat and 2 g saturated fat per ½-cup (125-mL) serving.

Caramel ice cream topping can be substituted for the Caramel Sauce, if desired.

When beating in egg whites and yolk, the cream puff mixture will at first appear lumpy, but will get smoother as you continue beating.

Piercing the puffs after baking releases the steam and helps ensure crisp cream puffs. Leaving the puffs in the oven for 5 minutes after baking will prevent them from deflating.

- 6 small firm ripe pears such as Bosc
- 1 orange
- 1 bottle (750 mL) dry red wine such as Cabernet Sauvignon
- 1 cup (250 mL) water
- ¾ cup (175 mL) sugar
- 2 cinnamon sticks
- ¼ cup (50 mL) seedless raspberry jam
- 3 squares (1 oz/30 g each) white chocolate for baking, coarsely chopped
- 3 tbsp (45 mL) fat-free half and half

Nutrition Facts

Serving Size 1 pear, 1 T sauce, 2 t jam
Servings Per Recipe 6

U.S. Nutrients Per Serving

Calories 230	Calories from Fat 45
	% Daily Value
Total Fat 4.5g	7%
Saturated Fat 3g	15%
Trans Fat 0g	
Cholesterol 5mg	2%
Sodium 20mg	1%
Total Carbohydrate 45g	15%
Dietary Fiber 5g	20%
Sugars 35g	
Protein 2g	

U.S. Diabetic Exchanges Per Serving

1 starch, 2 fruit, 1 fat (3 carb)

Wine-Poached Pears with White Chocolate Sauce

A few simple ingredients come together to create this elegant dessert.

PREP TIME: 10 MINUTES   **TOTAL TIME:** 6 HOURS OR OVERNIGHT
YIELD: 6 SERVINGS

1 Trim bottoms of pears, creating a flat base. Peel pears using **Vegetable Peeler**. Zest orange using **Zester/Scorer**. Combine pears, zest, wine, water, sugar and cinnamon sticks in **(4-qt./3.8-L) Casserole**. Bring to a simmer over medium heat. Reduce heat to low and simmer, uncovered, 40-45 minutes or until pears are tender and easily pierced with a knife. Remove Casserole from heat; cool to room temperature, about 20 minutes. Cover and refrigerate until completely chilled, at least 6 hours or overnight.

2 When ready to serve, place jam into **(1-cup/250-mL) Easy Read Measuring Cup**. Microwave on HIGH 30-45 seconds or until warmed; stir until smooth. Set aside.

3 For sauce, combine chocolate and half and half in **Small Micro-Cooker®**. Microwave, covered, on HIGH 30-45 seconds or until melted and smooth, stirring every 20 seconds. Carefully remove pears from poaching liquid; discard liquid. Blot pears dry with paper towels. Spoon 1 tbsp (15 mL) of the sauce onto each serving plate. Place pears over sauce; top each with 2 tsp (10 mL) of the jam. Serve immediately.

Cook's Tips

Letting the pears cool in the poaching liquid helps to impart even more of the flavor into the pears.

The pears can be prepared a day ahead. Keep refrigerated in poaching liquid until ready to serve.

RECIPE INDEX

No-Bake Desserts

Berry Granita Parfaits, 121

Espresso Panna Cotta, 111

Summer Fruit Ice Molds with
    Fresh Raspberry Sauce, 119

Wine-Poached Pears with White Chocolate Sauce, 125

One-Dish Meals

Creamy Saffron & Asparagus Risotto, 9

Lean 'N Green Thai Stir-Fry, 95

Spicy Mussels with Angel Hair, 41

Tomato-Herb Halibut en Papillote, 87

Pasta & Noodles

Chicken Farfalle Pomodoro, 99

Curry Chicken with Warm Fruit Compote, 39

Grilled Halibut with Soba Noodles in Asian Broth, 73

Grilled Sea Scallops with
    Roasted Red Pepper Couscous, 61

Lean 'N Green Thai Stir-Fry, 95

Lemon-Chicken Scallopine with Gremolata Orzo, 85

Mediterranean Lettuce Wraps, 57

Pan-Roasted Tofu with Sweet & Sour Noodles, 59

Skinny Turkey Tandoori, 89

Spicy Mussels with Angel Hair, 41

Sweet Potato Gnocchi with Bacon & Fresh Sage, 43

Tuna Cannelloni with Tomato-Caper Relish, 23

Wasabi-Glazed Ahi Tuna with Rice Noodle Salad, 65

Zucchini Ribbon Primavera, 91

Pastries & Pies

Cream Puffs with Caramel Swirl Ice Cream, 123

Decadent Chocolate Mousse Pie, 105

Raspberry-Chocolate Truffle Triangles, 117

Pork

Herb-Crusted Pork with Figs & Port Wine Sauce, 47

Korean Pork Tenderloin with Kimchi Slaw, 97

Watermelon & Prosciutto Salad, 21

Potatoes

Apple-Glazed Cornish Hens, 75

Smoky Yukon Gold Potato Chowder, 71

Spicy Poblano Burgers, 53

Surf & Turf Skewers with Grilled Potato Salad, 37

Sweet Potato Gnocchi with Bacon & Fresh Sage, 43

Warm "Meat & Potato" Salad, 63

Poultry

Apple-Glazed Cornish Hens, 75

Autumn Wild Rice Salad with Chicken, 69

Chicken & Goat Cheese Quesadillas with
    Papaya Salsa, 33

Chicken Farfalle Pomodoro, 99

Chicken, Green Bean & Apple Salad, 11

Chicken Sausage & Herb Wheat Pizza, 79

Chicken with Fresh Herb Chimichurri, 55

Crunchy Asian Chicken Salad, 49

Curry Chicken with Warm Fruit Compote, 39

Guiltless BLT Salad, 25

Lemon-Chicken Scallopine with Gremolata Orzo, 85

Loaded Baked Tomatoes, 29

Mediterranean Lettuce Wraps, 57

Skinny Turkey Tandoori, 89

Southwestern Tabbouleh Burritos, 67

Sweet Potato Gnocchi with Bacon & Fresh Sage, 43

Turkey Wonton Soup, 83

Rice & Grains

Autumn Wild Rice Salad with Chicken, 69

Baked Falafel with Jerusalem Salad, 27

Chicken with Fresh Herb Chimichurri, 55

Creamy Saffron & Asparagus Risotto, 9

Grilled Polenta with Vegetable Ragout, 45

Korean Pork Tenderloin with Kimchi Slaw, 97

Loaded Baked Tomatoes, 29

Quinoa-Stuffed Portobello Mushrooms, 19

Southwestern Tabbouleh Burritos, 67

Sweet Corn Cakes with Creole Shrimp, 51

Salads

Autumn Wild Rice Salad with Chicken, 69

Baked Falafel with Jerusalem Salad, 27

Chicken, Green Bean & Apple Salad, 11

Crunchy Asian Chicken Salad, 49

Fresh Herb Salad with Grilled Salmon, 81

Guiltless BLT Salad, 25

Korean Pork Tenderloin with Kimchi Slaw, 97

Surf & Turf Skewers with Grilled Potato Salad, 37

Sweet Corn Cakes with Creole Shrimp, 51

Tangy Citrus Salmon with Beets & Watercress, 93

Warm "Meat & Potato" Salad, 63

Wasabi-Glazed Ahi Tuna with Rice Noodle Salad, 65

Watermelon & Prosciutto Salad, 21

Shellfish

Cool Crab Cocktails with Mango Puree, 17

Grilled Sea Scallops with
    Roasted Red Pepper Couscous, 61

Grilled Shrimp Pitas with Basil Aioli, 13

Spicy Mussels with Angel Hair, 41

Surf & Turf Skewers with Grilled Potato Salad, 37

Sweet Corn Cakes with Creole Shrimp, 51

Soups

Cool Gazpacho with Watermelon, 31

Smoky Yukon Gold Potato Chowder, 71

Turkey Wonton Soup, 83

Tofu

Lean 'N Green Thai Stir-Fry, 95

Pan-Roasted Tofu with Sweet & Sour Noodles, 59

Notes on Nutrition

The recipes in this cookbook follow the general principles of good nutrition based on established public health and nutrition organizations such as the American Heart Association® (www.heart.org) and the United States Department of Agriculture (www.usda.gov)*. More detailed information regarding healthy diet and nutritional recommendations can be found by visiting AHA and USDA Web sites. It's important to keep in mind that the recipes in this cookbook can be included in a healthy diet when considered in the context of a daily or weekly meal plan.

The dietary information in this cookbook is not intended as a substitute for any dietary regimen that may have been prescribed by your doctor. As with all exercise and dietary programs, you should get your doctor's approval before beginning.

Here are the target ranges for maximum nutrient values that we used on a per-recipe basis in this cookbook**. Remember, the key is balancing food choices throughout the day to achieve the recommended daily guidelines.

	Calories	Total Fat (g)	Saturated Fat (g)	Cholesterol (mg)	Sodium (mg)	Carbohydrates (g)
Little Dishes	250-300	5-10	3-5	20-25	480	45
Main Dishes	500	10-15	5-7	60-150	500	45-60
Desserts	200-300	10	5-7	60	n/a	30-45

**Some recipes include foods that naturally fall outside these ranges but can be included in a healthy meal plan along with fruits, vegetables and whole grains. For example, shrimp are high in cholesterol but low in saturated fat and calories. Although the fat content of salmon is higher than our recommended range, it is high in "heart healthy" fats.

About Our Recipes and Generating Nutritional Information

All recipes in *Make It Fresh, Make It Healthy* were developed and carefully tested in The Pampered Chef® Test Kitchens. For best results, we recommend you use the ingredients indicated in the recipe.

We based our recipe development and nutritional analysis on the following:

- **Fresh vs. Processed:** The emphasis in this cookbook is on fresh ingredients, but when we did use processed foods (such as canned tomatoes), we tried to choose products labeled "light," "reduced" or "low." Reading the nutrition food label is important to make healthy decisions and to find items that will produce the best-tasting results.

- **Sodium/Salt:** We used reduced-sodium, low-sodium or unsalted products. At times, a pinch of table salt was used for flavoring.

- **Meats:** We used the leanest cuts of meat possible with all visible fat removed.

- **Marinades:** We measured and calculated nutritional information based on the amount of marinade that was absorbed into the food.

- **Oils:** The recipes in this cookbook call for low saturated oils such as olive, canola or sesame oil; however, corn oil (low in saturated fat) can be used.

- **Optional Ingredients:** Garnishes, fat used to grease pans, or serving suggestions are not included in the nutritional analysis.

- **Nutritional Analysis:** Nutritional analysis for each recipe is based on the first serving yield whenever a range is given and the first ingredient listed whenever a choice is given.

The nutrient values for each recipe in this cookbook were derived from The Food Processor SQL, Version 10.6.0 (ESHA Research), or are provided by food manufacturers. In addition to listing calories, total fat, saturated fat, cholesterol, carbohydrate, protein, sodium and fiber, we include two items commonly used by people with diabetes: diabetic food exchanges and carb choices. This information is based on the most current dietary guidelines, *Choose Your Foods: Exchange Lists for Diabetes (formerly Exchange Lists for Meal Planning) Sixth Edition, 2008*, by the American Diabetes Association® and the American Dietetic Association. Always consult with your physician, registered dietitian or certified diabetes educator, who will address your individual needs.

A Note on Canadian Nutrition

Nutrition guidelines vary in Canada. Nutrition fact panels are based on U.S. information. Visit Canada's Food Guide online at www.healthcanada.gc.ca/foodguide for more information.

* Mention of specific companies, organizations or authorities does not necessarily imply endorsement by The Pampered Chef®, nor does mention of specific companies, organizations or authorities imply that they endorse The Pampered Chef® or this publication.